The Pelican Guide to the Ozarks

Other Pelican guides

Big Bend Country
Gardens of Louisiana
Hillsborough: Historic Orange County, North Carolina
Historic Homes and Sites of Revolutionary America
Vol. I: New England
Louisiana Capitol
New Orleans
Old Homes of Mississippi
Vol. I: Columbus and the North
Vol. II: Natchez and the South
Plantation Homes of Louisiana
Virginia

The Maverick Guide series

The Maverick Guide to Australia
The Maverick Guide to Hawaii
The Maverick Guide to New Zealand

The Pelican Guide to
The Ozarks
By
Bet Hampel

PELICAN PUBLISHING COMPANY
GRETNA 1982

Copyright © 1982
By Bet Hampel
All rights reserved

Library of Congress Cataloging in Publication Data

Hampel, Bet.
 The Pelican guide to the Ozarks.

 (The Pelican guide series)
 Includes index.
 1. Ozark Mountains region—Description and travel
—Tours. I. Title. II. Title: Guide to the
Ozarks. III. Series.
F417.09H35   917.67'10453   81-17742
ISBN 0-88289-220-7   AACR2

Map of the Ozarks region by Max A. Gilbert, Arkansas Department of Parks and Tourism
Photographs courtesy of Department of Parks and Tourism, State Capitol, Little Rock, Arkansas

Manufactured in the United States of America

Published by Pelican Publishing Company, Inc.
1101 Monroe Street, Gretna, Louisiana 70053

Contents

TOUR 1: Fayetteville Area   9

TOUR 2: Eureka Springs Area   22

TOUR 3: Branson Area   32

TOUR 4: Joplin Area   44

TOUR 5: Lake of the Ozarks Area   52

TOUR 6: Lebanon Area   62

MAP   64-65

TOUR 7: Eminence—Big Spring Area   73

TOUR 8: Twin Lakes Area   80

TOUR 9: Mountain View Area   96

TOUR 10: Harrison Area   107

TOUR 11: Greers Ferry Area   115

INDEX   123

In grateful appreciation to all the wonderful Ozarkians who so generously provided the necessary information to compile this guide, especially the Arkansas Department of Parks and Tourism and the Missouri Parks and Recreation Department for the photographs of this area unsurpassed in beauty.

*This book is dedicated to my husband Carl
and our six children, Pat, Mark, Nancy, Sammie, Tim, and Mary,
who have made my travels through life perfect in every way.*

TOUR 1

Fayetteville Area

Plan to establish headquarters in the area surrounding Fayetteville, Springdale, or Rogers, Arkansas, in order to take full advantage of the many sights and attractions offered in this corner of the Ozark Mountains. These three cities virtually join boundaries, making one twenty-five-mile-long metropolitan area along U.S. Highway 71. Make your reservations early as the many motels, hotels, and resorts are filled to capacity most of the year.

The whole area is a vacationer's dream with easy access to nearby attractions plus the added historical significance of early Ozark settlements and Civil War battle sites. Feel free to strike out on your own as side roads are good and most drives quite scenic.

First to explore are the historical wonders found in Fayetteville. Begin with a tour of Headquarters House, located a half block off of U.S. Highway 71 on East Dickson Street. Admission is inexpensive and the tour very interesting.

See where a minie ball drilled its way through a door during the Battle of Fayetteville in 1863. Take the time to admire the fine period furniture gracing the old home. Walk around the corner to view the Butterfield Stage Line Marker before you leave the grounds, and be sure to pick up information on the other antebellum homes and historical markers to be found in Fayetteville.

To continue your historical quest, next visit the Confederate Cemetery. Follow Highway 71 south to Rock Street, turning three blocks to East Mountain. The thirty-five-foot-tall bronze statue of a soldier at parade rest welcomes you to one of the most interesting of all Civil War memorials.

Take a short tour of the old homes and markers by traveling across Highway 71, continuing on Rock Street to Locust Avenue. A historical marker tells of the Female Seminary, a school for Cherokee Indian girls. Turn north on Locust, driving past the Walker-Stone house built in 1847; see also the Ridge House across the street. Turn back east now on Center Street and you will pass still another old home, Reiff House, which was built in 1847.

Returning to Dickson Street, turn west to the University of Arkansas campus. Twin towers mark the location of the Old Main Building. Built in 1875, Old Main is now listed in the National Register of Historic Places.

Park your car and walk Senior Walk, reading some of the names of graduates from 1876 to the present time. Next you will want to view the extensive mineral, early American pressed glass, and pottery collections located nearby in Hotz Hall. The University Museum also displays Indian artifacts and fossils that have been discovered in Arkansas archeological digs.

If you are visiting this area in early fall, take advantage of the antique show or arts and crafts fair, both of which are held in Fayetteville. Check locally for the exact dates.

Set aside a full day for exploration of the area of Springdale and points west, circling back to Fayetteville.

Begin your tour with a visit to Shiloh Museum, located a few blocks from downtown Springdale. The museum, at 118 West Johnson Avenue, charges no admission. A curator and archeologist are on hand between the hours of 10:00 and 5:00 Tuesday through Saturday to conduct guided tours.

Take your time sifting through the more than 25,000 artifacts of the man-made history of this area. There are displays of early pioneer tools, furniture, and clothing. Examine the pioneer doctor's bag complete with all his crude instruments. Enjoy viewing the rare books, glassware, early calling cards, handwoven coverlets, almanacs, antique sidesaddles, and fancy women's bonnets as well as the miniature scenes of pioneer homes. And be sure to see the Indian burial brought intact from a nearby bluff and placed on display in the museum.

One absolute must during your visit is a taste of famous Southern fried chicken. Stop for an early lunch at any of the restaurants featuring this delicacy.

After lunch, turn west onto Highway 68, noting the lush grape vineyards along the highway as you approach the tiny Italian village of Tontitown. An annual Grape Festival, celebrating the grape harvest, is held during the month of August; be sure to attend if you are in the area, as this is a festival to be remembered.

Continue on Highway 68, passing through a corner of the Ozark National Forest, and study the scenery of this lovely area.

You may want to stop next for a visit in the town of Siloam Springs. This was a famous health resort at the turn of the century and boasts twenty-eight free-flowing springs. Enjoy a leisurely stroll through this tiny town, stopping to admire the old buildings, which are still in use today. Be sure to have a drink of Arkansas spring water before leaving on Highway 59 south.

Traveling along the Oklahoma-Arkansas border, stop to enjoy the scenic views. Turn back east on Highway 62, continuing the loop drive. One mile east of Lincoln, the highway travels through the middle of apple orchards, bringing you to Appletown, U.S.A. Stop here for a refreshing drink at the Red

Apple Cider Saloon. Push through the swinging doors and sidle up to the bar for a free shot of fresh apple cider. Have your picture taken with one of the mannequins dressed as a gunslinger, bar maid, or piano player. Then saunter out back for a look at the giant cider press that makes 1,500 gallons of cider a day. The saloon is open from 8:30 to 5:00 daily during apple season, July to January.

Visit the apple butter plant and country store. Then have an apple dumpling with free coffee or a dish of homemade ice cream. You may also want to purchase apple cider, apple butter, apple blossom honey, or cider candy to take home as a souvenir. Amble on over to the Appletown Smoked Meats Store and pick up a stick of summer sausage or a dill pickle on a stick before continuing along Highway 62.

History buffs will want to turn south on Highway 45 to Cane Hill, site of two early colleges, the first Sunday School in this area, and the county's first corn grinding mill. Others may proceed to the Prairie Grove Battlefield Park, where they can spend the rest of the day exploring the interesting and entertaining site. Tour the unique collection of pioneer buildings depicting life from the 1830s to 1860s. The museum in the park is open daily except Mondays from 10:00 to 4:30. Here you can relive the famous battle fought in December 1862.

A visit during the first week of September would enable you to see the Prairie Grove Clothesline Fair. The fair features oils, watercolors, photographs, hand-painted china, and many other interesting displays for your browsing pleasure. Then rejoin Highway 62 for the return to Fayetteville and Springdale.

For your evening entertainment, you might wish to take advantage of the summer musicals featured at the Arts Center in Springdale. Other seasonal entertainment the visitor might enjoy includes a rodeo July 1 through July 4 and the annual poultry festival in Springdale during the spring.

Plan another full day for the exploration of the area to the north and east, beginning at the city of Rogers. Be sure to carry your fishing gear and camera for a day of relaxation, fun, and scenic beauty.

The International Air Gun Museum, at the Daisy Heddon Company, is a one-of-a-kind museum depicting the history of the air rifle. Free to all, the museum is open for tours weekdays 9:00 to 5:00. You might also enjoy a plant tour available each weekday at 1:30.

Before leaving Rogers, stop at the market on U.S. Highway 71 for a look at how country hams and bacons are cured the old-fashioned way. Try several free samples, and, if you wish, order sandwiches to take with you.

Beautiful Beaver Lake, sprawling through the Ozark Mountain Range, features every possible aquatic sport. Here you may enjoy several hours of relaxing fun: spread a picnic on the shores or rent a party barge for a perfect outing. Drop a hook into the water, for many known types of fish, including bass, catfish, and crappie, bite regularly here. The hundreds of secluded inlets and coves also offer a perfect place for boating, skiing, swimming, and drifting.

You can reach the shores of Beaver Lake via Highways 264, 94, 12, and 127. After fishing, hike the nature trails or simply enjoy the beautiful views. For the hunter, the dense forests abound with game in season.

During the afternoon, take U.S. Highway 62 northeast of Rogers ten miles to the Pea Ridge National Military Park. Make a point to attend the excellent educational slide show presented by the National Park Service in the visitor center. The most important Civil War battle west of the Mississippi River was fought here in 1862.

Follow the seven mile self-guided tour tracing the progress of the opposing forces in this battle that saved Missouri for the Union. Walk through Union and Confederate trenches on a bluff overlooking Little Sugar Creek. Drive past impressive monuments and cannons. Examine Elkhorn Tavern, the only remaining building that served both forces. Stop for a moment at the spot next to the tavern where the Butterfield Stage passed on its cross-country route between St. Louis and San Francisco. The visitor center is open daily from 8:00 until dark and there is no admission charge.

On your return to the Springdale-Fayetteville area, travel some of the more remote backwoods country. Follow Highway 62 back into Rogers, then turn onto Highway 12 heading east, passing over the beautiful, clear waters of Beaver Lake. Follow Highway 12 until it intersects with Highway 45, winding south down through the magnificent Ozark Mountains. Turn back to the west on Highway 68 leading toward Springdale.

Soon the highway intersects with Zion Road, where you will find an informative marker of the old Butterfield Stage Route. Turn south on Zion until you join the Old Missouri Road, and later the Old Wire Road. You will be traveling the old stage route into Fayetteville.

An attraction not to be missed in this area is the annual Ozark Arts and Crafts Fair held at War Eagle Mills Farm in October. This 142-year-old farm is located along the banks of War Eagle Creek between Highway 12 and Highway 68 on Arkansas 303.

There is no admission charge for the fair. Over 400 craftsmen from all over the Ozarks display their wares in three giant tents. All entrants are severely screened so you are assured of only the very highest quality crafts. Take your choice of original oils and watercolors, hand-painted china, or handwrought jewelry. Examine the pottery, wooden ware, carvings, oak and hickory baskets, and character dolls. Purchase furniture or accessories fashioned from native woods, such as walnut, cherry, pine, or oak. There are also Ozark recipe books,

Old Main Building, University of Arkansas (Fayetteville, Arkansas)

home-preserved jams and jellies, and old-time soaps and sachets. Be sure to go to the fair early, because this event draws thousands of visitors each year. You may bring your own box lunch or purchase a good country-cooked meal on the grounds. An old mill and small museum add to the enjoyment of the visit.

For a tour of the area to the north and west of Rogers, take Highway 71 leading to Bentonville. Stop at the tourist information booth to check dates for local folk festivals, crafts fairs, or fishing tournaments.

Follow Highway 72 leading 3½ miles west to the Civil War Cave. The cave features many beautiful and natural pools, which were once used as water supply for the Confederate troops. You may tour the cave any day of the year until dark. Admission is charged.

Continue on Highway 71 north of Bentonville, passing through the beautiful village of Bella Vista. Local golf courses are fantastic.

Follow Highway 71 north out of Arkansas into Missouri, where it intersects with Missouri Highway 90. Take 90 west leading to Noel, where you will find the Bluff Dwellers Cave, a one-mile natural wonder shaped by water. A tour lasts forty minutes, and is available between the hours of 8:00 and 6:00 daily. Stop by the museum display of rocks, minerals, arrows, skeletons, and antiques before beginning the return trip into Arkansas.

Follow Highway 59 south, returning to the Rogers-Springdale-Fayetteville area via Highways 72, 102, 68, 12, 16, or 62, all leading east.

Get an early start for a full day of interesting, exciting, and historic attractions as you travel south and west of Fayetteville.

Highway 71, tumbling down through the gorgeous Boston Mountain Range, will carry you approximately six miles to the town of West Fork.

Turn here onto Highway 170 which will lead you a short distance to the SEFOR Nuclear Experiment Station. If the visitor's center is open, take an educational tour and then browse through the interesting and entertaining models and displays regarding the peaceful use of nuclear power.

Be sure to load your camera as you continue south on Highway 170 winding down into Devil's Den State Park. In this remote recreation area, you can hike gorgeous nature trails and explore caves and crevices. You might wish to return another day to swim, fish, or picnic. Or you might want to camp on the overnight hiking trail.

Highway 74 leading east from the park entrance will take you through the town of Winslow. Historically, this was once a major stop on the Butterfield Stage Route. Today there are roadside stands of local crafts for your browsing pleasure.

Turn south onto Highway 71 following the beautiful Talimena Skyline Drive across some of the highest peaks in the Ozark Mountains. The luscious odor which permeates the air comes from a local smokehouse where you will most certainly want to stop for a leisurely lunch.

Then continue on to Artist Point where you may saunter through the Indian Museum, and the craft and gift shop. Take the trail down the mountainside, viewing the Indian Burial Mound, the Deer Foot Slide, and the phenomenal Balanced Rock. Before returning to the museum, stop to see the Indian icebox, Horse Tail Falls, and Lover's Leap.

Next cross Highway 71 and follow the arrows that lead down the winding gravel road to the bottom of a rugged Ozark valley. To the right is the ghost town of Schaberg, once the site of the Frisco Line turntable. To the left, the road will carry you across a creek to a remote native stone and log house, where you will find exceptionally talented woodcarvers turning out original horses, cowboys, animals, birds, and other unique works of folk art.

Return to Highway 71 south. Lake Fort Smith and Lake Shepherd Springs are both easily accessible to the east of the highway. Surrounded by the majestic Ozark Mountain peaks, they each offer unsurpassed scenic beauty, as well as swimming, fishing, and picnicking.

Travel through Mountainburg to the junction with Interstate Highway 40, turning west into Fort Smith.

In the early 1800s Fort Smith was the last stronghold of civilization on the western frontier. Separated from Indian Territory only by the Arkansas River, Fort Smith was a refuge for notorious outlaws, such as Belle Starr. You can still see some of the gambling casinos and brothels, such as Pearl Starr's infamous boarding house.

In the late 1800s, the "Hanging Judge," Isaac C. Parker, brought law and order to the Indian Territory. His courtroom and the nearby gallows tell the story of his reign.

Begin your tour of the nineteen historic interest points at the Fort Smith National Historic Site, where you can gather information plus directions to all the other sights. To reach the historic site, travel down Fort Smith's main street, Garrison Avenue, which was once the parade ground for the fort's troops. Turn one block south on Second Street to Rogers Avenue. Judge Parker's courtroom and a museum featuring pioneer relics are open daily from 8:30 to 5:00. During July, a gun show is held in Fort Smith, but you will need to check locally for exact dates and times.

Try to leave Fort Smith in early afternoon so as to enjoy the return trip to Fayetteville. Travel first through the beautiful old town of Van Buren, also listed as a National Historic Site. Stop to see the Albert Pike School House, situated on the Crawford County Court House grounds.

Turn onto Highway 59 north, relishing the scenery as you move through the Ozark National Forest. Twenty miles north of Fort Smith is the black shale Natural Dam, found only a few hundred yards off the highway. The ten-foot-high dam appears to have been man-made, but is actually a phenomenon of nature. You will want to walk the natural sidewalk across the top of the dam, viewing the many waterfalls below. Slip off your shoes and wade in the tranquil pool of icy waters of Mountain Fork.

Then follow the country road to the top of the nearby hill, where you have an excellent photographic site commanding this lovely area. Search the grounds for Indian relics and momentos of the Civil War era.

Continue on Highway 59, following the Arkansas-Oklahoma state line to the junction with Highway 62, which will lead you east into Fayetteville.

Another adventurous day will carry you southeast from Fayetteville on Highway 16 to its junction with Highway 23. Turn south onto 23 winding down through the luxurious, indescribable beauty of the dense Ozark National Forest.

An unpaved road to the west will take you sixteen miles deep into the forest for rugged mountain scenery, spectacular bluffs, rim trails, and hunting in season at White Rock Mountain. Farther along on Highway 23, another unpaved road will carry you to Shore Lake on the Mulberry River for swimming, boating, fishing, floating, hunting, and sightseeing at Devil's Canyon and Deep Hollow.

Continue your scenic drive south on Highway 23 to the junction with Interstate Highway 40. A few miles to the east is the small mountain village of Ozark. Here you may watch a string of barges being locked through on the Arkansas River.

Drive a few miles farther east on the Interstate to Exit 41, which will take you to the summit of St. Mary's Mountain. The vineyards, the chalets, and spectacular scenery at the top of the hill produce the feeling of alpine adventure.

Elkhorn Tavern (Pea Ridge, Arkansas)

Judge Parker's Court (Fort Smith, Arkansas)

Tour the winery here, making a special visit to the wine tasting room. Then enter the restaurant where the costumed waitresses and candle-lit tables provide the atmosphere for German-Swiss cuisine. Enjoy the complimentary glass of wine as you listen to the alpenhorn background music.

The restaurant is open 11:00 to 2:00 and 5:00 to 9:00 Monday through Saturday. You may also tour the vineyards, if interested. The tours of the winery are available from 9:00 to 1:30 Monday through Saturday. There is no admission charge for the various tours.

Before returning to the highway, stop at St. Mary's Church atop the mountain for a bit of historical sightseeing.

You may return to the Fayetteville area via Clarksville to the east; follow Highway 64 from Altus to this peach market of the foothills. An annual peach festival is held in Clarksville at harvest time, usually during July.

Follow Highway 21 north through the timbered area of the Ozark National Forest. At Fallsville, take Highway 16, which cuts through some of the most scenic areas of this beautiful land. Highway 16 will return you to the Fayetteville area.

You may prefer the ease of the Interstate 40 route west from Ozark to the junction with Highway 71 north. If you have time, you might wish to make a return visit to Devil's Den State Park for a leisurely few hours of relaxation, perhaps including a cookout, before returning to the Fayetteville area.

TOUR 2
Eureka Springs Area

Majestic Victorian style homes, three stories tall, perched precariously on the mountainsides; a church with the main entrance through the belfry; and over seventy "healing" springs flowing unceasingly from deep inside the mountains. Such are only a few of the attractions of the "Little Switzerland of the Ozarks," Eureka Springs, Arkansas.

Located on Highway 62, the isolation of Eureka Springs makes it a true Ozark vacation paradise. Plan to spend at least several days exploring its many attractions.

Eureka Springs is situated on two parallel mountain ridges, with the business section located in the valley below. Its entire business district is on the National Register of Historic Places.

At the very top is the completely restored castle in the sky, the Crescent Hotel, where the elegant of the gay nineties lodged while taking advantage of the mysterious waters which the Indians believed held healing powers. You may wish to begin a tour of the city from here, either riding or walking down the mountainside.

Stop first at St. Elizabeth's Catholic Church, once featured in Ripley's Believe It or Not, as having its main entry through the bell tower.

Next stop on the side of the mountain is the hobby center where each item displayed is a handmade original. Be sure to purchase a hickory nut doll or a genuine homemade sun bon-

The Rosalie (Eureka Springs, Arkansas)

Unusually built homes (Eureka Springs, Arkansas)

net as a souvenir of your visit to this unique Ozark hide-away.

Turn next onto Spring Street where you will see the Rosalie, a gingerbread encrusted Victorian home. The small admission charge will entitle you to a leisurely stroll through the fully restored, antique filled rooms.

As you continue down the hillside of Spring Street, note the Basin Park Hotel, another of Ripley's features, having seven floors, all on ground level.

Stop at the base of the mountain for a drink of the delectable spring water. Remember to come back to this spot any summer night except Saturday and Sunday for a free hillbilly show.

Watch for the 1885 vintage trolley. Plan to ride a few blocks or farther sometime during your day.

At the intersection of Main and Spring streets is the Historical Museum, housing a collection of books, pictures, and articles depicting the history of this Ozark region.

Turn right onto Flint Street for a short visit to the Carrie Nation Hatchet Hall, last home of the temperance crusader of the early 1900s.

Returning to Main Street, drift into the various craft shops, where original jewelry made from stones of the area, as well as many other handmade items are displayed. Be sure to make a visit to the local country store where you might purchase Ozark smoked sausage, smoked hams, homemade relishes, jams or jellies to take back home as reminders of your visit.

Top off your day with a visit to the doll museum.

You may wish to board a free bus for your trip back up the mountainside to your hotel, motel, boarding house, or dormitory. All of these types of lodging are in plentiful supply. The influx of tourists during the summer months makes it always advisable to have reservations well in advance. Eureka Springs is definitely not an attraction to merely pass through. The roads are crooked and hilly, though all are in good shape.

Because of this, the trip into and out of Eureka Springs takes longer than the average drive.

A day of interesting sightseeing awaits you to the south of Eureka Springs. Just a few miles from the city limits on Highway 23, you will find the strangest stone dwelling of the Ozarks. Walls are constructed of unusual Ozark rocks, and the rooms are completely independent of the outer walls. Exotic plants grow two stories high between the floors and the walls. It is well worth the small admission charge.

Continue still farther south and follow the signs leading to Hog Scald Hollow, a rock collector's paradise. The admission entitles you to explore the area where both Confederate and Union soldiers slaughtered wild hogs and cooked them in the natural kettles provided by nature. The isolation and dense foliage of the area seem to carry you a century away from the busy world.

Plan to stop for a picnic at Withrow Springs State Park where a concession stand is open during the summer months. Also found nearby is a custom woodcrafting and folk art center, where original furniture and quilts are produced.

Retrace your steps to Eureka Springs, taking time to enjoy the unspoiled natural beauty of the Ozark Mountains. Stop along the way to photograph the more spectacular scenes before you.

Dine this evening in the Victorian atmosphere of one remaining bath house from another era. Located on Spring Street, this dining room is quite popular.

Travel to the west of Eureka Springs on Highway 62 for another fun-filled day. Bring your camera along and pack your fishing gear for an angler's treat later in the day. As you travel, watch for Pivot Rock and Natural Bridge. Both are natural wonders formed from Ozark rock. Admission is charged.

A little way to the west is the Miles Mountain Musical Mu-

Country Store, Inspiration Point (Eureka Springs, Arkansas)

The Church in the Wildwood

seum featuring a unique collection of rare and antique musical instruments and music boxes. You will be treated to musical entertainment from days gone by, as well as a tour of the museum. You will also enjoy browsing through the clocks, paintings, and carvings. The museum is open daily 9:00 to 5:00.

Lake Leatherwood, only four miles west of the city, features picnic areas, campsites, swimming, fishing, and boating. Seven miles west, turn off the highway to Inspiration Point. Here atop Rock Candy Mountain, the scenery is gorgeous. Young musicians come here each year to study and perform. You may take advantage of their concerts and operas during the season.

Take a guided tour through the replica of a German castle situated high above White River. Tours are available daily 9:30 to 5:00. Then browse through the country store and antique shop. See the blacksmith shop and the old time "filling station."

A few miles beyond Inspiration Point on the same access road is one of the world's largest springs. Beautiful, clear Blue Spring produces thirty-eight million gallons of water each day. The spring is of historical significance, being situated on the Cherokee "Trail of Tears." You may want to photograph the Indian writings on the cliffs above the spring. Children may feed the trout and ducks that abound in the spring waters. Admission is charged.

Return to the main highway, continuing west a few more miles. You may want to stop at the museum of dolls along the way.

Then turn onto Access Road 187 to the beautiful Beaver Dam and Lake. Haul out your best fishing gear when you reach the lake. The black, white, and striped bass, crappie, bream, channel cat, northern pike, and walleye bite in the many secluded coves of the lake.

Below the dam area, the icy cold waters of White River hold rainbow trout, almost waiting for your line. All public facilities are free of charge, thus making this a true vacation paradise for the swimmer, hiker, spelunker, fisherman, or boat enthusiast.

Continuing west on Access Road 187 another two miles brings you to Dinosaur Park. Here you will find excellent campsite accomodations at reasonable prices. Enter the park on a swinging bridge that spans a creek and waterfall.

The park is dotted with life-sized prehistoric figures including a giant boa constrictor fashioned from a huge grape vine. Besides the unusual features of bag swings, tree houses, and a real dinosaur factory, you may enjoy feeding the thousands of trout that swim beside a pavilion.

Return to the highway via 187, turn left, and travel farther west to the Pea Ridge National Military Park only a few miles away. Here a very decisive Civil War engagement took place in 1863. Enjoy the slide show in the visitor center and then follow a self-guided tour of the battlefield. Stop to see the Elkhorn Tavern, the only surviving building of that conflict.

Another full day of fun is to be found north of Eureka Springs. Travel Highway 23 to the town of Beaver, just a few miles away. Here you can enjoy delightful fishing, swimming, and boating on beautiful Table Rock Lake. In addition, there is a delightful cruise an the lake and an animal park nearby, where animals are trained for movies and television.

To explore the area farther north, take a tour to Roaring River State Park, located in the Missouri Ozarks just twenty miles away. The tours are particularly delightful in spring and fall, when the foliage is in its fullest development.

To the east of Eureka Springs are still more and different attractions. The first of these is the Church in the Wildwood. For the admission, you can see the world's largest collection of Bibles and sacred artifacts. Another mile to the east takes

Christ of the Ozarks

Scene from Great Passion Play

you to Onyx Cave, formed entirely from onyx. Admission entitles you to explore all five magnificent rooms of the cave.

As you emerge, look to the east where the giant seven-story Christ of the Ozarks statue dominates the skyline. With armspan of sixty-five feet, the statue is almost indescribable in monumentality and beauty. The statue may be seen throughout the year, and admission is free to those of all faiths.

Drive along the mountain ridge to the entrance of the statue where the Christ Only Art Gallery is located. Here may be seen nearly 400 portrayals of Christ, depicted in every known art form. Admission is minimal. The Great Passion Play, presented on a huge stage in a natural amphitheater beneath the statue, is presented from late May to late October, five nights a week at 8:30.

Continuing to the east, stop at the nearby Kings River. Make advance reservations to float this beautiful Ozark stream on another day when you can fish, photograph, sightsee, or just simply lie back and drift lazily downstream through the magnificent Ozarks.

A few miles farther east is the town of Berryville where the Saunders Memorial Museum houses guns representing the history of arms in the United States. See the personal handguns of Billy the Kid, the James Brothers, and Poncho Villa, along with the collections of antique furniture, china, and silverware. Hours are 9–5 spring through fall.

Next stop is the Carroll County Museum and Heritage Center located in the historic Carroll County Court House. View the tools, equipment, furniture, clothing, and dishes from another era.

Berryville also boasts a rodeo in July, a county fair in September, and a muzzle loading gun shoot complete with wagon train in the fall.

Turn onto Highway 21 North from Berryville and travel

eight miles to Cosmic Cavern. Here you can take a thirty-five-minute tour to see the world's longest underground bridge, the Ozark's largest underground lake, and the beautiful frozen milkyway.

Stop in the gift shop to browse through the carved onyx pieces and the other rocks and crafts offered for your souvenir purchases. The nearby picnic area is free to all.

Summer fun in Eureka Springs also includes an antique show, an arts and crafts show, and an antique car show.

The Ozark Folk Festival held during the fall months features parades, a Gay Nineties Revue, and a Barefoot Ball where the requirement for dancing is checking your shoes at the door. Check locally for exact dates and times for all festivities.

Before leaving Eureka Springs, include a visit to the art gallery located in the old schoolhouse.

Finish off your visit by dining in antebellum elegance at the New Orleans Hotel. Built in the late 1800s, the hotel is listed in the National Historical Register and the atmosphere is marvelous. Another suggestion is to return to the mountaintop for Victorian luxury in the dining room of the Crescent Hotel.

TOUR 3

Branson Area

Wear your sneakers and pack all your fun gear as you head for the entertainment-filled area surrounding Branson, Missouri. Reservations are a must; this area of the Ozark Mountains attracts many visitors throughout the year.

With the three lakes and the surrounding mountain ranges, the scenery is marvelous. Picturesque scenes greet you at every moment of your trip into this exciting, yet wonderfully relaxing part of the world.

A variety of attractions are offered here—more than enough to satisfy your every desire. You can hike or ride a helicopter, fish or ride a speed boat over the beautiful clear lakes, or simply remain a bystander, watching all the sights. Horseback riding, fishing, water skiing, golf, sailing, boating, scuba diving, and stage shows are only a few of the many diverse types of entertainment you can expect in this area.

Plan to set up headquarters in or near Branson, along Highways 13, 76, 165, 265, or 65. There are fabulous resorts or tent camping areas. Motels, lodges, hotels, and housekeeping or sleeping cabins abound on every side. Most lodges or resorts offer free freezer service for the limit of fish you hope to catch. Some offer playgrounds, pools, and baby sitting services. Tennis or golf are included with some accommodations. Others offer free boats and motors.

For pure excitement, Silver Dollar City should be your first day's outing. Arrive at the gate before 9:00 A.M. in order not to miss a single moment of fun.

There are two differently priced tickets. The higher priced one is the best buy as it includes repeat visits to all of the attractions, crafts, shows, and historical sights you can possibly squeeze into one day-long outing; the lower priced ticket excludes some of the major attractions. Head right for the heart of this 1880 Ozark town where you can walk the boardwalks and watch demonstrations of those native crafts handed down through the generations.

Glassblowers and glasscutters shape glassware before your eyes. The donkey turns the sorghum mill, just as it was done many years ago. Stop for a visit with the Horse and People Doctor. Tour the McHaffie Homestead with its smokehouse out back. Stop to sit for a moment on a pew in the Wilderness Church where services are held each Sunday morning at 10:00.

Grab a snack at the outdoor market and take a float trip in a johnboat on a lazy Ozark stream. Watch as old-fashioned lye soap is made outdoors. Taste the apple butter as it comes from the pot. Then take a ride on the stagecoach as it bumps and jogs you along the trail through the remote countryside.

Gather your family together and have a tintype photo made. Then have your name printed in a newspaper at the Print Shop. Grab an ice cream cone on your way to chase the Baldnobbers Gang through "Fire-in-the-Hole."

Rest for a moment in the gazebo in the center of the park. Then tour more of the craft displays. You will see candles made just as the original Ozarkians made them; watch as pottery is formed; purchase a basket or broom to take home with you.

Then watch the commotion as Carry Nation and her hatchet-wielding cronies march toward the Silver Dollar Saloon where can-can girls dance on the bar in high-topped boots, tights, and multi-colored petticoats. Hop on the Frisco Silver Dollar Line and rest your feet as you ride the steam-powered locomotive through the backwoods. Be careful that you aren't robbed as you pass through some of the more remote spots. Have a hillbilly sandwich before traveling through the Flooded Mine and climbing up the Treetop House. Walk through Grandfather's Mansion—if you can.

Then set aside an hour to tour the fabulous Marvel Cave. Tours begin every thirty minutes. You ride the Cave Railway deep down into the earth to the chamber twenty stories high, where your tour begins. You will see a huge waterfall deep beneath the earth's surface. The vastness of this cave is astounding.

Return to the park and join in the fun of the Hatfield-McCoy Feud or the 1880 Military Retreat Ceremony. Both of these evening entertainments are staged during the peak summer months. Or take in a show as the sun begins to set behind the trees. Have dinner in one of the restaurants on the grounds. All feature some form of hillbilly cooking. Make sure to purchase some homemade candy for dessert.

May, June, September, and October are excellent times for a visit to Silver Dollar City. During these months, a ticket purchased after 4:00 P.M. will entitle you to return the next day for more fun and frolic.

The park is open from 9:00 A.M. to 8:00 P.M. during the summer months. During spring and fall, the hours are 9:30 A.M. to 6:00 P.M. each day except Monday and Tuesday.

The month of June offers a festival of mountain folks' music. At that time, you can join with the Ozarkians in a little foot-tapping and singing as they play their dulcimers, jawbones, jew's harps, guitars, banjos, and autoharps.

The National Festival of Craftsmen is held here beginning in September and running into October; this is the ideal time to view the marvelous changing of the trees in the surrounding hills. All of the native crafts are displayed and demonstrated during this festival, including rail splitting, cornshuckery, meat smoking, sand casting, and fiddle making. You will also see rope making, yarn dyeing, silversmithing, and seed pictures.

Turn onto Highway 76, which leads west from Branson, dipping into the rolling Ozarks. One mile west is a frontier town, complete with a museum for your inspection.

You can take a ride in a helicopter, viewing the lush Ozark Mountains in one quick swoop. Or you can ride the "ducks," which carry you along over the land and the water to show you the nearby sights.

Amble along at your own pace, taking delight in the many attractions offered in this marvelous wonderland. You may wish merely to drive about the Shepherd of the Hills Country, made famous by Harold Bell Wright's book.

There are four entertainment theaters in a row along the highway. All four feature excellent Ozark family entertainment nightly during the summer months. Check locally for show times and specific attractions. One tends to barbershop and gospel, another bluegrass, and the other two, country humor and music. Take your choice or plan to see all four for good entertainment at a reasonable cost. One of the theaters features a talent contest in the fall.

An amusement park along the highway offers rides and an arcade. Next is an Indian museum where you can view artifacts from this Ozark area. Across the way is Jim Lane's Cabin, the homestead of one of the main characters from *The Shepherd of the Hills*. There is also a nearby reptile garden, which has live exhibits and an evening show for a different type of entertainment.

Around the bend is Dewey Bald Mountain, which figures prominently in Harold Bell Wright's story. Across the highway is Mutton Hollow, the peaceful, quiet nook described so beautifully in the story. Today it is filled with the same peace and quiet, the same remoteness from the world. There is no admission charge to this area.

Take time to walk along The Trail That Nobody Knows How Old. Tour the Shepherd of the Hills Farm where Old Matt's Cabin stands. Sit on the porch and watch as the world passes by. Make reservations to see the Shepherd of the Hills Play at the Old Mill Theatre on the farm. Then take one of the jeep drawn tours of the whole area in order not to miss a single important fact or place in this story of a time gone by. The tours leave every few minutes all summer long.

See Inspiration Point where Harold Bell Wright camped while writing this remarkable story. Hike the nature trails through the area or ride horseback through the rolling hills. Stables are located at the farm and in Mutton Hollow.

Next visit the Wash Gibbs Museum also located on Highway 76. Then see Uncle Ike's Post Office, another important historic site in the famous book.

Late in the afternoon, turn onto Highway 76–60, which drops down along a peninsula with the waters of Table Rock Lake lapping on either side. Haul out your fishing gear, your swimming suit, or your picnic supplies and spend a couple of hours relaxing on the beaches. You can even rent a tent if you decide to spend the night in this quiet area of the Ozark Mountains.

Table Rock is one of the finest bass fishing lakes in the country. The smallmouth and spotted bass come on long stringers in whopping sizes. Boat docks in the area have all equipment for rent if you have forgotten something. Scuba divers will want to return to this peninsula another day for interesting dives in the quiet, cool waters of the magnificent lake.

Return to Shepherd of the Hills Farm in time to have a steak cooked over an open fire. Then walk the Trail That Nobody

Knows How Old once again before showtime of the evening's outdoor pageant of this famous story.

Another full day's entertainment awaits you as you circle from the south around Branson. Pack your fishing gear and camera and travel south to Hollister on Highway 65. Plan to spend several hours casting a line for the hungry rainbows on upper Lake Taneycomo. Fishing is year round in this area and there are no mosquitoes to hinder your fun. If you would like to contract for a one-day float to chase after these luscious trout, there are boats and guides available throughout the area.

Ice down your catch and travel a little farther south on 65 to the unique School of the Ozarks, where every student works his way to a college degree. Load your camera and hop on the free Campus Special, which will tour you around.

You will see the Friendship House, Williams Chapel, and the famous ninety-six-bell carillon in the Bell Tower. Stop at Edwards Mill, where students grind corn meal with a buhrstone. Then spend some time viewing the historic firearms, Indian collection, and coin collection to be found in the Ralph Foster Museum. The tearoom and the cafeteria are available for meals on the grounds. Plan to return one evening during the summer months for a performance by the students at the Beacon Hill Theatre.

Continue on Highway 65 to its junction with 165. Take 165 leading into the Table Rock Dam area. It will be an enjoyable scenic drive with the lakeshore on one side and beautiful Baird Mountain on the other. Stop to view the dam where the powerhouse is open to visitors on weekdays. Then tour the trout hatchery below the dam. It is open every day throughout the year.

Continue along the lakeshore on Highway 265, driving through the Falls Creek area. Here you will find secluded fishing coves with fish waiting in every one. View the model

Williams Memorial Chapel, School of the Ozarks (Point Lookout, Missouri)

Edwards Mill (Point Lookout, Missouri)

railroad and artifacts of this area. Purchase a snack to enjoy as you travel leisurely through the hollows and hills that make up this fascinating countryside. Watch the afternoon shadows as they dance along the blue grey ridges, dipping down through the dark green forests. Follow 265 to its junction with Highway 76, where you will retrace your steps of yesterday back into Branson.

Another day-long adventure lies north and west of Branson, beginning on Highway 248. You will need your camera to record the fantastic scenery. And of course you should always carry your swimming duds and fishing gear. You never know when to expect a swimming hole or a fishing cove.

Travel up Highway 248, stopping to enjoy the view from Cula Vista a few miles from Branson. Then continue on the sideroad to the left, where you will find an old sycamore log church. Continue to follow 248 to Reeds Spring Junction. Turn here onto Highway 160, which will carry you to the Old Spanish Cave, another of the Ozark's wondrous holes in the ground.

Return to the junction, turning west along Wilderness Road. You are now traveling the same trail that the James Gang, the Daltons, Youngers, Quantrill's Raiders, and even Bonnie and Clyde once traveled. All the original settlers of this Ozark region once traveled along this Old Wilderness Road.

Stop at the clock museum to browse through the wide variety of handcrafted grandfather clocks and mantel pieces. Also a mini-craft show is in continuous operation along this road throughout the summer months.

Leaving Wilderness Road, turn south onto Highway 13, riding the ridges to Talking Rocks Cavern. You will be amazed at the unusual formations left by nature. The tour is well worth the admission.

If you have time, you may want to turn onto Highway DD,

a fabulous camera route. The entire peninsula is one of perfect scenic beauty. White Rock Bluff offers a spectacular view of the lake stretching out below.

Arriving in Kimberling City on Highway 13, you might have time to rent a houseboat or smaller rig for an afternoon of pure pleasure on bass-filled Table Rock Lake. If not, you can still fish from the dock, hike the nearby nature trails, or laze away the afternoon on the sandy beaches.

Later in the evening, ride the excursion boat that departs from the Highway 13 boat dock. Enjoy dinner aboard while gliding lazily along the clean, calm waters. As the evening comes to a close, return to the Branson area along the now familiar Highway 76.

A longer trip to the west of Branson will provide you with the perfect lazy day of nothing to do but fish, picnic, hike, and enjoy slow-paced sightseeing.

Set out early, following Highway 76 to Reed's Spring, where it then turns west. Stay on 76 as it crosses Table Rock Lake and then plunges down through the rolling hills and deep valleys of the Mark Twain National Forest, affording you many spectacular views. Stop along the way to take photos of the more beautiful sights.

Arriving in Cassville, tour the trout hatchery before driving to Crystal Caverns one-half mile north of town on Highway 37. After touring the cave, head straight for the best trout fishing imaginable in Roaring River State Park. Travel into the park via Highway 112 south from Cassville.

This is one of the most beautiful areas of the Ozarks. Campgrounds are beautiful, picnic areas perfect, and cold, clear mountain waters cascade without end down over the bluffs. Purchase a one-day permit and hurry to drop your hook in the water. Then stand on the banks and reel the trout in.

Spread your picnic lunch on the green grass, lean back against a tree, and let the world pass you by. Or you might cook your catch over an open fire in the wilderness. Hike through the woods; pick wild flowers. Enjoy the solitude of the area. Then pack up your gear and drive along Highway F, which will carry you across the park to Highway 86.

As you pass through the Eagle Rock area, watch for items made from native walnut or cedar. You may happen on to one of the festivals with apple butter making, meal grinding, or corn shucking. There is an amusement park offering a few minutes of fun.

Follow Highway 86 as it crosses Table Rock several times on your scenic drive back to Highway 65, where you turn north into the Branson area. Pack another picnic or stop to pick up a box lunch as you take your fishing gear and head for beautiful Bull Shoals Lake to the east of Branson. The gigantic ten-to-twelve-pound largemouth bass are waiting for your line.

Travel Highway 86, turning off on Highway K or MM, both of which lead directly to the lake. Highway K offers several boat docks where you may rent all fishing and water skiing equipment. Highway MM leads to a marina where you can put your own boat into the water for a few perfect hours on this clear, calm lake.

Besides the famous largemouth, you can also get your limit of smallmouth, white spotted, and warmouth bass, walleye, crappie, bluegill, and the fighting channel and bullhead cat.

Scuba divers will want to spend several hours exploring the depths of these quiet, clear waters. This area also offers swimming, horseback riding, excellent hunting in season, canoes, paddle boats, and the ever popular pontoon boat tours.

In some places, you can pick up excellent lunches designed for your all-day fishing pleasure. Resorts abound, some offering hay rides, cookouts, trail rides, freezer service, and general family accommodations.

If you prefer, you may travel further into the Bull Shoals

area, taking Highway 160 where it junctions with 86. Follow this scenic route through the tip of the Mark Twain National Forest, driving south on any of the access roads leading to the lake. Or continue on Highway 160 to Highway 125. Turn south on 125 for perfect rock hunting, bird watching, hiking, or picnicking. Then ride the free ferry across the beautiful waters, crossing into Arkansas on the other side.

Returning to the Highway 86–160 junction, be sure to stop in to see the reconstructed old-time pioneer homestead, which is open during the summer months. Cross the bridge and take Highway Y-10. Circle around the pot hole area at the dam site, view the dam, and then tour the powerhouse. Drive past the beaches and rejoin Highway 76 at Forsyth. If the white bass roundup and fish fry is being held while you are visiting, be sure to take advantage of some of the hearty eating.

Continue to follow Lake Taneycomo, turning onto Highway EE, which will take you into the Rockaway Beach area. The amusement parks are open all year round. There are also snack bars and swimming beaches for your fun-time pleasure. Be sure to take the cruise to further explore the winding, snake-like Lake Taneycomo.

A crafts and antiques show is held here in June each year, and a show followed by a fireworks display is held each Fourth of July. Another annual festival is featured during the fall months. Check locally for exact dates in order to take advantage of some of these special events.

Take Highway 76A to rejoin 76 and then return to the Branson area via Highway 65.

In Branson, another scenic cruise on Lake Taneycomo will offer you several hours of delightful entertainment. You are carried on a fifteen mile cruise to pick up the daily supply of gold from a mine in the area. On the return trip, you just might be robbed by the Pirate of Taneycomo. There are two tours daily; be sure to book one of them for scenic beauty plus plenty of laughs.

Then visit the White River Museum at the boat dock before heading for a dinner of famous White River catfish or scrumptious trout, served up with local cider and topped off with honey from the Ozarks.

Tour 4

Joplin Area

If you have time for only a taste of the Ozark Mountains, then by all means visit the Joplin, Missouri area. With the plains of Oklahoma stretching out to the west and the Ozark Mountains rising to the east, the Joplin area offers you every possible entertainment. Although Joplin boasts many motels and hotels, reservations are a must for any portion of the Ozark Mountains.

Leisure clothing for sightseeing, fishing equipment, swimming accessories, and of course a loaded camera are all in order for your trip around this western tip of the beautiful Ozark Mountain wonderland.

First tour the world famous Tri-State Mineral Museum located in Schifferdecker Park between Fourth and Seventh Streets. Examine samples of the various minerals native to this mining district. Then see the displays of mining methods and equipment used over the years. As you leave the museum, be sure to snap a picture of the beautiful Grand Falls located in the park. The museum is open Tuesday through Saturday from 10:00 to 5:00 and on Sundays from 1:00 to 5:00.

Another museum located on Main Street offers still further insight into the rich heritage of this region.

A day full of sightseeing entertainment is to be found south of Joplin, beginning with the George Washington Carver National Monument. Travel Highway 66 west of Joplin a few miles to the junction with Alternate Highway 71. Turn south to Diamond, Missouri. Then follow the signs leading to the National Monument Visitor Center and Museum honoring this famous black scientist.

The surrounding park is kept in its natural state. Walk the mile-long nature trail past the important points in his boyhood. The park is open daily 8:30 to 5:00.

Continue on Highway 71 south, rolling down through the foothills to Neosho, nestled in the lush green fields of the Ozark plateau. Sometimes referred to as Flower Box City, Neosho features beautiful flowers throughout the year. There is also a colorful living flower clock in Big Spring Park. Beautiful trees fill the hills with splendor. The bright colors of fall are particularly breathtaking.

An Arts and Crafts show is held each Sunday afternoon in Neosho park. Visit between the hours of 1:00 and 6:00 during the summer and fall months.

Returning to Highway 71 south, travel another few miles to the small community of Anderson.

Visit the local craft shops, and watch as jewelry is fashioned from area minerals and wild flowers. You can even make your own jewelry in some of the shops.

Stop in the nearby area for a rock hunting expedition of your own. Try to find a crystal, fossil, or perhaps an Indian weapon to take home as a souvenir of your visit to this special corner of the Ozarks.

Next stop will be for a snack of some of the cheese made in the local plant. Check for times of tours of the plant.

Hunting for quail, small game, and deer in season is excellent in this plateau area.

Grab a light wrap now as you are about to be treated to four equally interesting, though very different caves as you continue traveling south.

The first is Truitt's Cave in Lanagan with hourly tours all

during the year. After a tour, you might want to have lunch in the quaint underground cafe. View the free "Believe It or Not" section and then continue on to the next cave.

Turn onto scenic Highway 59 south toward Noel, Missouri. Follow the signs to the beautiful Ozark Wonder Cave only one-half mile from the highway. You will enjoy the forty-five-minute tour of this cave as you view seven rooms of multicolored onyx. The annual "Little Spelunker Days" is held each October. The cave is open all year and well worth the admission and your time.

As you wind your way down through the magnificent Overhanging Bluff Drive on Highway 59, you approach still another attraction, Mount Shira Cave. Not as commercially developed as the others in the area, this one is still worth a stop.

Spelunkers will especially enjoy this section of the Ozark Mountains. There are nine mapped caves to explore at your own risk.

Stop for a moment of relaxation at Pineville where you might want to take a canoe ride across the junction of the Big and Little Sugar Creeks. Then continue on your scenic drive through the mountains, crossing the bridge over Elk River into the town of Noel. The Elk River Lake nearby features gravel beaches for swimming and boating enjoyment.

The rivers and lakes in this area offer great fishing for smallmouth and largemouth bass, channel and bullhead cat, and the prized golden red horse sucker.

Two miles south of Noel, visit the Bluff Dwellers Cave for a mile-long guided tour. The cave is open all year and admission is quite reasonable. You will want to browse through the museum.

Turn to the west now along beautiful Highway 90, leading to Southwest City, Missouri. Pose for a picture while standing in three states at the cornerstone that marks the Mason-Dixon

Portrait of George Washington Carver

Apple Butter Makin' Days (Mount Vernon, Missouri)

Line.

Turn back north towards Joplin, traveling along picturesque Highway 43. Stop at Elk River, taking a while to drop your line into the waters in the cool evening shadows. Then stop somewhere along Highway 43 to enjoy a scrumptious dinner of fresh catfish.

You will enjoy another day of sightseeing to the east of Joplin. Travel along Highway 44, scanning the north side of the highway for a glimpse of the day lily and peony fields in bloom.

When you cross Spring River, stop for a tour of the Chesapeake hatchery before continuing on into Mt. Vernon. Here you will want to try a sample of native apple butter. If you visit during the fall, you will see apple butter being made in copper kettles out on the courthouse square.

During this time, the surrounding hills are bathed in glorious color of the Flaming Fall Revue. Any time of the year, you will find the forests are magnificent. Summer brings lush greens, spring offers pink and white dogwood and redbuds, and winter shows stark, ice covered branches against the rugged hills.

In Mt. Vernon, turn south on Highway 39 toward Aurora. The area surrounding Aurora is noted for its particularly beautiful trees throughout the year. Reload your camera for some truly beautiful shots to remind you of your visit to this lovely nook of the world. An old fiddler's contest, held here in September, offers you the opportunity for some foot stomping and hand clapping.

Turn back to the west on Highway 60 and travel to Monett. Spread a picnic lunch in the park while the children fish in the well stocked lake designed just for them. The nearby U.S. Weather Radar Station may be open for your inspection.

Travel across the ridges to the west and turn north onto Highway 97, proceeding two miles to Pierce City. Here you can see Harold Bell Wright's church, which he founded before he wrote his famous works. The library holds the original key to the church where he began his preaching career.

Continue west on Highway 60, stopping to see both the Jolly Mill and Ritchey Mill on opposite sides of the highway. Cross Alternate Highway 71 and continue into Neosho, where you join the Ozark Frontier Trail Highway 71, which will carry you back into Joplin. Spend the rest of your afternoon fishing along Shoal Creek for bass, crappie, sunfish, or catfish.

Then enjoy a hillbilly supper of hickory-smoked ham and beans. Square dancing, little theatre performances, and activities at the malls are all enticing evening attractions.

Carry your fishing gear and camera with you as you travel to the north of Joplin on another interesting daylong adventure.

Take Interstate Highway 44 to its junction with Highway 71 north leading into Carthage. You will first want to drive slowly past the beautiful, castle-like Jasper County Courthouse, a recognized landmark in this portion of the Ozarks.

Inside the courthouse are several museum cases containing relics of the Civil War and other items that make interesting viewing. You may see these between the hours of 8:00 and 5:00 weekdays. Also look for the plaques on the square marking the birthplace of the infamous Belle Starr, and honoring ragtime great James Scott.

Many important Civil War battles were fought in and around Carthage. Watch as you travel for markers telling the stories of these battles.

Sightsee the town, enjoying the vast display of Victorian-era architecture in the old homes. You will also want to take time to search for antiques in the many shops. You might try some French dressing or barbeque sauce, both of which are made locally.

Spring River, which runs through the town, features excellent fishing. You may make reservations for a float to see more of the spring. Largemouth bass, smallmouth bass, white crappie, green sunfish, catfish, and golden red horse sucker can all be found in this clear mountain stream as it winds lazily through the Ozark bluffs.

Before leaving Carthage, you will want to see the world's largest gray marble quarry on the northern outskirts of town.

Travel north of Carthage to the town of Lamar. Load your camera for a snapshot of the modest white frame home where Harry S. Truman was born on May 8, 1884. Take a short walk around the grounds and pose before the flag pole. See the completely restored home, complete with period furnishings. A gift shop is adjacent to the site.

Then continue farther north to the town of Nevada, twenty-five miles away. This area was the site of several bitter Civil War battles. Relics can still be found among the hills, valleys, and river bluffs that mark this western edge of the Ozarks.

It was here that the hated Order No. 11 was issued, forcing Southern sympathizers to leave their homes within fifteen days. Many items from these frightening days are housed in the Buschwhacker Museum in Nevada. For a small admission, you can spend several hours reliving history.

Travel now along to the east on Highway 54, crossing Clear Creek to El Dorado Springs. Have a pleasant lunch here in the mineral spa area.

All of this area offers good hunting and fishing. Duck hunting is particularly good in the area north of Highway 54. The bass are waiting in Clear Creek and Horse Creek nearby.

Turn south on Highway 32 to the Stockton Lake area where you will then turn onto Highway 39 south. Enjoy the scenic drive beside the lake, stopping among the hills to have a snack or relax as you travel along.

On the southern edge of the lake, rent a sailboat, fishing rig, or ski rig for an afternoon entertainment. Take a dip in the lake before leaving for more interesting sightseeing.

The Greenfield Museum, just a short distance south of the lake, was built in 1867. See the displays of earlier days in famed Dade County, Missouri. Daniel Boone's rifle and many other interesting items make this stop a must on your tour. The museum is open April through October, weekdays 10:00 to 6:00.

Continue south on Highway 39 to the junction with Highway 66 west, which will carry you back to Carthage in time to tour the site of the Battle of Carthage, one of the most important of Civil War battles.

Have dinner at one of the many restaurants featuring true Ozark hickory-smoked hams or sausage. Then spend the evening at the Memorial Hall, where square dances are presented each Tuesday night year round.

You will want to save one full day to float Shoal Creek south of Joplin. Make arrangements in the Joplin area. Then grab a boat and your fishing gear and spend the whole day doing nothing but drifting and enjoying the beautiful scenery and the perfect fishing offered here in this magnificent Ozark country.

TOUR 5

Lake of the Ozarks Area

If your plans call for spectacular scenery, relaxing water sports, interesting caves, and reasonably priced entertainment, then the Lake of the Ozarks should be your destination.

You will find family accommodations throughout the area. There are also plush lodges, housekeeping cabins, motels, hotels, condominiums, and campgrounds. Some provide free boats and accessories for the length of your stay. Others provide free freezers for your catch, baby sitting services, playgrounds, sandy beaches, and even private baited crappie beds for that little extra fishing pleasure.

Reservations are required, no matter what season you visit. The peak vacation months fill the area to capacity with tourists. Most lodging units offer special rates for the spring, fall, and winter seasons, thus attracting an equal number of off-season visitors.

The magnificent scenery, changing at every bend of the road, literally takes your breath away. Sky blue waters, sandy beaches, and green hills combine to offer excellent photographic sites. Be sure to bring your camera and plan to carry it with you on each excursion.

Lake of the Ozarks is located on U.S. Highway 54 and Missouri Highways 5 and 42. Accommodations can also be found on all the smaller access roads leading into the lake area.

Begin your various tours of the lake area from the Bagnell Dam, located on Highway 54 at Business Route 54. First take a free tour of the dam offered any weekday beginning at 9:30 A.M. and on Sundays and holidays beginning at 8:30 A.M.

Circle through Lake Ozark on Business Route 54 for a five-mile treat of souvenir shops, crafts, and entertainment. Shop through the authentic Indian jewelry, pottery, dolls, and rugs. Amble through the wax museum to see the life sized outlaws of the Jesse James era. Stop in to watch the glassblower, candlemaker, or other craftsmen as they go about their daily tasks.

Let the children ride the go-carts and mini-bikes on the nearby tracks. Then have a sandwich made from open pit barbecue and spend a few hours lazing the time away on the public beach. Ride the pedal bikes or yaks, enjoy the free swim tubes, or just watch and enjoy the clear blue waters.

Farther down on Highway 54, visit the factory that makes the cedar souvenirs found here. Take a free tour any day 9:30 to 3:00.

Next visit the Missouri Aquarium only a mile below the dam. Let the fish eat right out of your hand.

Returning to the dam site, be sure to take a ride out over the beautiful trees on the chair lift. Enjoy the eagle-eye view of the lake and the beginning of the Ozark Mountain range.

Purchase a ticket for a cruise on the beautiful sky blue waters. Cruises are offered every hour from 10:00 A.M. to 8:00 P.M. You might prefer to save this treat for later in the evening when the dance cruises are offered at 9:00. There is also an additional cruise Saturday evenings at 11:30.

Take a helicopter or seaplane flight out over the lake at anytime during the day. All of these various tours leave from the dock next to the dam.

Plan to attend the Ozark water ski show sometime during your visit. Performances are presented at 8:30 nightly or each

Bagnell Dam and Lake of the Ozarks

The Angel's Shower, Ozarks Caverns (Osage Beach, Missouri)

afternoon at 2:00.

Still more entertainment in the form of dancing or shows is offered along the strip adjacent to the dam later in the evenings.

A day long adventure awaits you to the north and west of the dam area. Bring your fishing gear as you begin your travels north along Highway 54. See the collection of antique guns just north of the dam. An annual gun show is held in the area during the month of June. Check locally for exact dates and times. You will want to take a short tour of Starks Cave, another of nature's wonders tucked away here in the Ozarks. Then continue on to Eldon. Relax for a few moments in the park or play a few holes of golf on one of their excellent courses.

Then turn west on Highway 52, leading into Versailles. Here you will enjoy a relaxing interlude as you tour the Morgan County Museum. Then walk the town square where you will see crafts, water colors, and oil paintings.

Have a snack of homemade candy before you travel south on Highway 5, stopping to tour Jacob's Cave, one of the more beautiful natural caves of this area. After you cross the bridge, turn right to travel a few miles to see Natural Bridge.

Then continue south through this more secluded section of the Ozarks. Stop next to tour the spring-fed trout hatchery. Nearby you can schedule a boat ride to take advantage of the peace and tranquility found in this area.

If you are an amateur at fishing, this is the ideal place to try your luck. Here you can fish for trout with a guaranteed catch. The more experienced fishermen can drop their lines into the local baited crappie beds for the sheer fun of a bite on every cast.

Adventurous hikers can strike out along the tree filled Ozark bluffs. The spelunkers can explore some of the local caves.

Continue traveling south, catching a glimpse of the waters of the lake as you weave along the Ozark ridges.

Stop in Laurie to purchase a supply of fried chicken, then head straight for the nearby coves where the fish are always biting. Spend the rest of your day hauling in bass, crappie, jack salmon, or channel cat. When the sun is too high for fishing, you can swim or ski. You might even prefer to just relax against a tree.

Later in the evening, drive into Sunrise Beach and ride the water bikes. Take your camera to Hurricane Deck, where the beautiful bluffs overlook the blue expanse of lake waters.

Return to Laurie and take a boat ride out for unique shopping and dinner. Then attend a live hillbilly musical held in Laurie at 8:30 P.M.

Return to your lodgings via Highway 5 south, turning onto Highway 54 north.

Plan another excursion south and west of the dam area. Drive on past Osage Beach and cross over the beautiful Glaize Bridge. Five miles further west will bring you to an authentic frontier town of the 1890s.

Hitch a ride on the stage. Duck as you pass the gun fight on Main Street. See the local blacksmith at work down at the livery. Have a shot of "corn whiskey" while can-can dancers pass before your eyes at the saloon. Ride the train, but hang on to your valuables. You just might get held up. Then have an ice cream at the local parlor. Stop at the trading post, take a trail ride through the backwoods, and finish up your visit at the old timer's museum. The town is open daily 10:00 to 6:00. Plan about two hours to enjoy all the sights.

Continue along Highway 54 south to Linn Creek, crossing another scenic bridge into Camdenton. Backtrack along Highway 5, crossing Highway 54 and following the signs to Bridal Cave, one of the most beautiful caves in this area. As you tour this onyx and dripstone wonder, you may be fortunate enough to attend one of the many weddings performed in the chapel before the magnificent backdrop provided by nature.

Climb the nearby tower for a look at this beautiful landscape. Then drive along any of the side roads in the area to get a better look at the surrounding waters. Picturesque bluffs overlook the lake on one side and the Niangua River on the other, creating the perfect site for a photograph to remind you of your visit.

A dogwood festival is held in Camdenton each spring, along with a local fishing derby. A square dance festival sets the tone in the month of June. Check locally for exact times and dates.

You may want to try your luck at sonar fishing from some of the local docks. There are guide services for help in finding the perfect fishing spot. All of this area abounds with water sports of all kinds, including fishing and swimming.

Return to the Osage Beach area and purchase your tickets for the local opry performance, to be held later in the evening. Have a delicious dinner of Ozark ham or summer sausage before showtime.

Pack enough food for a day. Gather up your fishing and swimming paraphernalia. Load your camera. Then follow Highway 42 east of Osage Beach, turning onto Highway 134, which leads you into Lake of the Ozarks State Park. Here you can enjoy a truly magnificent day doing absolutely nothing but loafing the time away.

Fish the crappie beds, swim the quiet coves, ride the speedboats, or ski the crystal clear waters. Then ride horseback through the quiet forests or hike the nature trails. Paddle a canoe through the shadowy waters beneath the sheer bluffs.

Spread your picnic beneath a shady tree. Take a nap on the thick green grass. Then spend the afternoon exploring the nearby caves.

Hike through the woods to Prairie Hollow Cave. Then take a boat across the lake to explore beautiful Ozarks Caverns. Return to climb Kaiser Tower for another spectacular view of the edge of the magnificent Ozark Mountain range. Then tour the fish hatchery in the State Park.

Have a cookout as the evening cools. Then fish from the banks as the catfish, crappie, and bass come up to feed.

Get an early start for another full day of sightseeing and fishing. Pack your best rig and your camera. Then head for truly spectacular fishing to the west of Bagnell Dam.

For a closer look at the back country of this border of the Ozark Mountains, travel Highway W, a paved two-lane road running across the hills to Versailles. If you prefer the main highways, travel Highway 54 north to Eldon, then west on 52 to reach Versailles.

Continue to the west through Stover, which boasts another fish hatchery. Turn onto Highway 65 at the Cole Camp junction. This will lead you to Warsaw, which juts out over the northern tip of Lake of the Ozarks.

Travel on through Warsaw, following Highway 7 west as it crosses over the magnificent expanse of waters where the Osage River and Pomme de Terre River join the lake. Then turn off on Highway KK, following the back roads to the banks of the Osage.

Rent a boat and hire a guide. Then bait your hook for the scrapping, battling, paddle fish or spoonbill cat that inhabit these remote waters.

After you have snagged some of these fighting wonders, hike the river banks and nearby woods. Search the ground for relics of the Osage Indians, who lived here many hundreds of years ago.

Stop nearby to eat some of that delicious fried catfish before leaving this unhurried section of the world.

Start your return trip to the main lake area by following

Missouri State Capitol (Jefferson City, Missouri)

Detail of mural, Missouri State Capitol

Highway 7 south. Wind across the ridges and down through the rich valleys. Pass through the villages of Majorville and Climax Springs.

Cross over the clear, rippling waters of Turkey Creek and Deer Creek. Ride alongside Dead Man's Ridge. And keep your camera poised every moment to record the more spectacular scenery.

Highway 7 junctions with Highway 5 which will take you into Camdenton. Then continue on Highway 54 north to your lodgings.

Another short side trip will take you to the state capitol located in Jefferson City just 45 miles northeast. Travel Highway 54 leading directly into the Capitol City.

Tour the state capitol and museum where you will want to view the famed murals which depict the history of Missouri. Other points of interest in the Capitol City are the executive mansion, Jefferson Landing State Historic Site, Cole County Historical Museum, and the State Highway Patrol Museum.

Shop the local malls or have a leisurely lunch of that famed country ham and red-eye gravy.

Return to the main lake area via Highway 63 east to its junction with Highway 133 south. Stop to tour the Rocky Valley Museum which features artifacts of the area. Admission is charged.

Cut over onto Highway 52, which will take you back into the Eldon area. Stop to view the natural bridge here on the Osage.

If you have a few extra moments, you might wet a hook in the river, savoring the peace and quiet of the area.

Continuing west towards the dam area, turn onto Highway V, which will take you to the Indian Burial Cave. Take a tour through this former home of Indians. See the fifteen-hundred-year-old skeletons. Then browse through the museum before traveling on to your lodgings.

If you still have time on your hands, be sure to ice skate in the huge nearby rink or ski the man made snow runs. Attend a rodeo, play golf, play tennis, take a sauna bath, or shop for antiques.

Be sure to set aside some leisure time for lolling in the sun on the sand beaches and just looking at the beautiful clear waters of Lake of the Ozarks.

TOUR 6

Lebanon Area

Hidden in the crevices of the Ozark hills, Lebanon, Missouri is a perfect midpoint headquarters for seeing the sights of the surrounding Missouri Ozarks. Make reservations early as this is a popular vacation spot year round. Be sure to bring a camera, fishing rod, and lots of spare time in order to thoroughly explore the many attractions offered to you in these beautiful mountains. Lebanon is located at the junctions of Interstate Highway 44 and Missouri Highways 32, 5, and 64.

For the first day's entertainment, gather up your fishing gear, swimming accessories, and casual clothes. Pack your camera and head for beautiful Bennett Springs State Park, only a few miles west of Lebanon on Highway 64.

Stop in the park to buy bait, license, and picnic supplies. Then wade into the icy waters, cast your line, and wait for the hungry rainbow to strike. You are almost guaranteed your limit as this stream is stocked daily. When you tire of fishing, picnic on the jagged banks and dangle your feet in the clear rushing waters.

After lunch, you will want to sign up for a short float down the Niangua River. There are several put-in points in the park. You may wish to float the river without a guide, however, guide service is available at the put-in points. Sit back in your johnboat, relax, and let the banks drift past as the river carries you to your take-out point.

If you should want to stay longer in the park, make reservations early for one of the housekeeping or sleeping units. You may also camp on the banks of the stream. As the day ends, have dinner in the lodge. Then attend a lecture at the nature interpretive center before returning to the Lebanon area.

For an entirely different sort of day, take your camera and get an early start for the two hour drive east along Highway 44 to the Meramac State Park area. You might pick up a bottle of real "Missouri Corn Whiskey" or perhaps some Ozark pottery as you travel along.

Turn off the highway onto Exit 215 at Leasburg to Onondaga Cave, America's second largest. Onondaga, an Indian hunting sanctuary, was discovered by Daniel Boone. The cave is open every day and charges a small admission.

After a tour of the cave, stop for a moment at the craft displays and souvenir shops. You can fish, picnic, boat, or camp in the park area. During the fall of the year, there is a unique rock-skipping contest.

Returning to Highway 44, travel a few more miles to Exit 230 at Stanton for a visit to the largest single cave formation in the world, Meramac Caverns. This cave is quite unique in that it encompasses five stories. Tours are led by rangers along well lighted walkways.

See the Underground Railroad station through which passed thousands of slaves in their bid for freedom during the Civil War years. The cave was also used as a powder mill by the Union forces during that time.

It was later used by the Jesse James gang as a hideout for both men and horses. After being cornered here, Jesse James is said to have escaped via an unknown passageway and eventually made his way to freedom. Be sure to see the Loot Rock and hear the story.

You will also want to stand beside the huge Stage Curtain, said to be the largest single cave formation in the world.

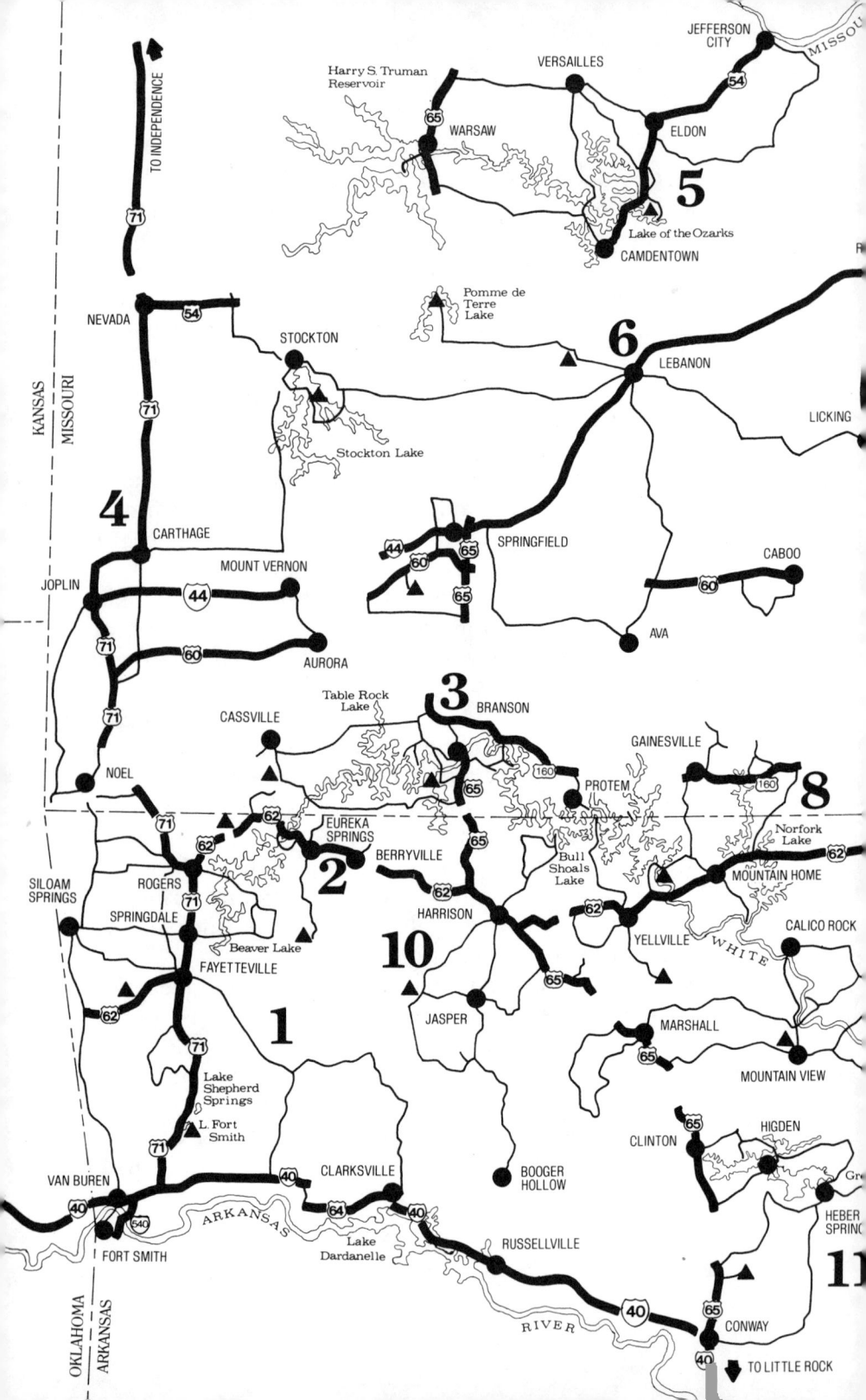

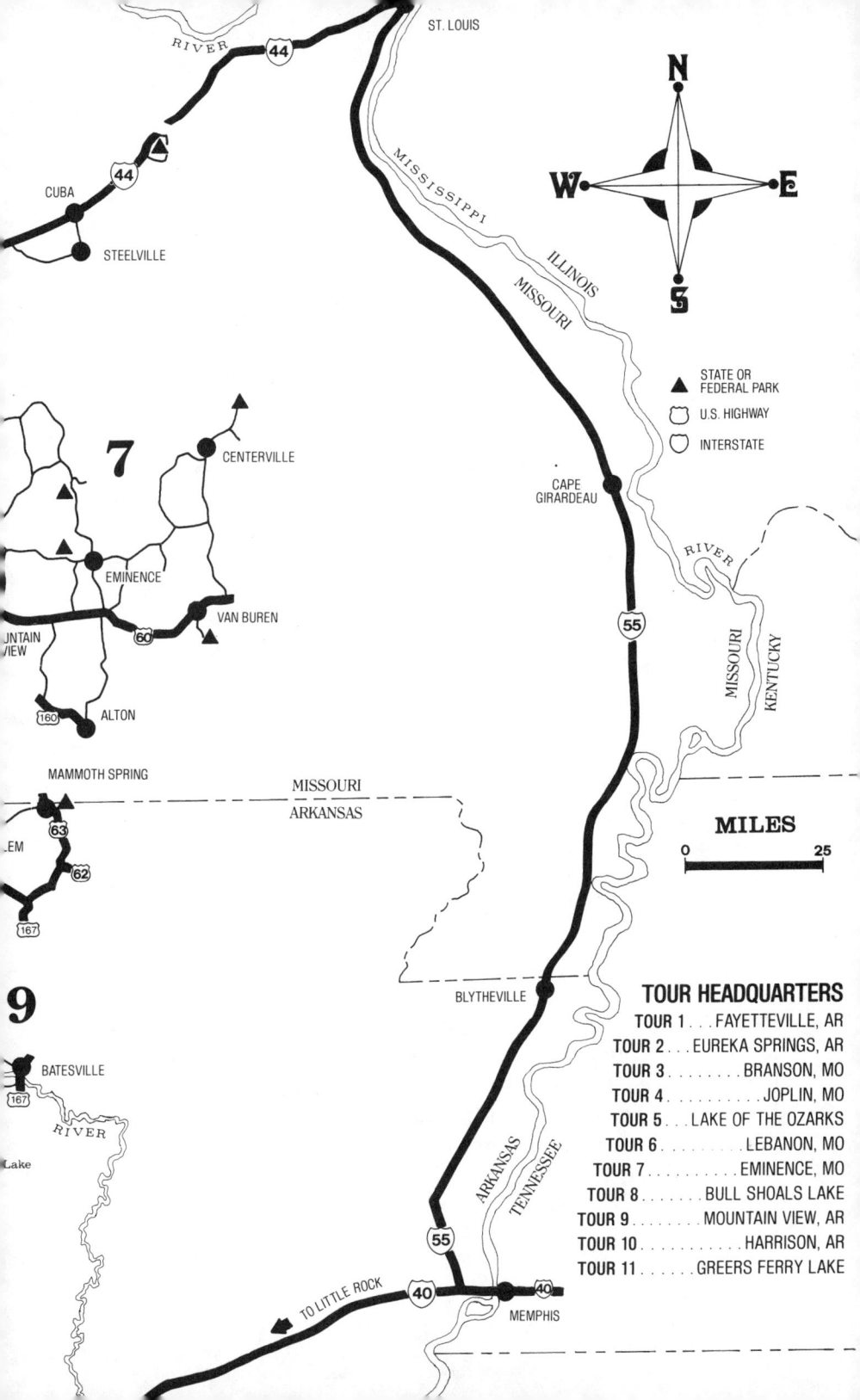

Observe the beautiful submarine garden and see the huge underground Auditorium Room, where various shows and dances are held throughout the year.

Above ground is the LaJolla Park with its many picturesque trees shading the picnic area. Fishing, boating, and camping are also available to you here on the Ozark River. A cafeteria and coffee house offer snacks or meals.

Take a tour through the nearby Jesse James Wax Museum where you will see and hear the story of Jesse's purported escape from the lawmen. He is said to have lived near here to the ripe old age of 103. Admission is charged.

If caves interest you, visit Fisher's Cave nearby in Sullivan.

Returning to the west along Highway 44, stop at the site of the Civil War iron furnaces. Drive past Cuba, turning onto Highway 19 and traveling to Steelville. Take Highway 8 west, which circles through the beautiful countryside to the iron furnaces. Then Highway 8 will carry you back to Highway 44. The opportunity to see the magnificent rolling hills of the countryside makes the trip worthwhile.

Stop at one of the many restaurants in Rolla for a bowl of country beans and ham. Then turn south onto Highway 63 for a memorable drive through the hills of the Ozarks. Stop a few miles south of Rolla at Yancy Mills, an old-time water mill on a branch of the Piney River.

Continue traveling south on Highway 63 to Licking. Turn west here onto Highway 32 for an unsurpassed scenic drive through the Ozark Mountains.

A few miles west of Licking, cross the Big Piney River. Stop here for a moment and look to the south to see the White Rock Bluffs. Further south, hidden from view, is the Balanced Rock, a true phenomenon of nature. Still further south is the beautiful area called the Narrows. You might want to take a float trip down the river for a better view; set aside time to make this excursion another day.

Continue west on Highway 32, passing along the rolling ridges and dipping down into the lush green valleys. The rugged hills surround you at every bend of the road. Stop often to take photos of this fabulous land.

You pass over the Gasconade and Osage Fork Rivers, both of which offer excellent fishing. Drop a line into any spot for smallmouth and largemouth bass, crappie, bream, and channel cat. A golden red horse sucker or the bullhead cat might challenge you to a real fishing match.

Hunting is also excellent throughout this area. Duck, squirrel, and quail, as well as deer and turkey, are in abundance in season.

Stop to explore Dry Nob Mill here on the Osage Fork. Then continue your return to the Lebanon area.

If you would like to make a short trip for magnificent fishing or hunting, travel to the Roubidoux Spring and Roubidoux Creek trout area just a few miles east of Lebanon on Highway 44. The Piney, Gasconade, and Osage Fork rivers form a network that fills the entire area with the finest game and fish imaginable.

An exciting full-day adventure awaits you south of Lebanon on Highway 44, in the Springfield area.

Travel first to the exotic animal paradise located twelve miles north of Springfield. For a small admission fee, you can drive your car through ten miles of fascinating animal wonderland.

Stay in your automobile with the windows up and photograph some of the 3,000 animals and rare birds that surround you. The Bengal tiger, Chinese leopard, American brown bear, zebra, ostrich, Hawaiian sheep, and even the Ozark mountain goat move lazily around your car as you creep along through the hills and valleys that make up their natural habitat. The park is open every day from 8:00 A.M. until one hour before sundown.

Continue into Springfield, traveling on 44 to the junction with Highway 65. This will carry you five minutes out of Springfield to Crystal Cave. This cave is unusual in that it exhibits such natural beauty that there is no colored lighting used. This will give you the opportunity to see a perfectly natural cave. The cave is open from May to November.

Another equally fascinating, yet entirely different cave adventure awaits you to the west. Take Highway WW, which will carry you a few miles west to Highway 13. Turn south on Highway 13 toward Springfield. A few miles farther along, follow the signs that lead to Fantastic Caverns. This is the only cave in the world large enough to drive all the way through. Purchase your ticket and climb aboard the jeep-drawn conveyance. Enjoy forty-five minutes of true wonderment and fun as the Ozark guide drives you along the underground trails. You will particularly enjoy the vast differences of color, ranging from pure onyx white to the deepest black.

After the tour, you might wish to have lunch in the free campgrounds or stop on the way into Springfield at one of the many restaurants that feature true hillbilly cooking.

As you travel throughout this area, be sure to pick up a folklore book listing some of the Ozark superstitions or purchase a true Ozark cookbook to use at home later. Both will offer many hours of pleasure.

Metropolitan Springfield offers varied and interesting attractions for a day of pleasure. There is an art museum with fine watercolors for browsing. Venture through one of the four college campuses. During the fall, Drury College sponsors a sidewalk art contest that is always interesting to attend.

The lakes of Springfield afford you an opportunity for sailing in the soft breezes, boating, swimming, or just plain loafing in the parks.

Shop the Battlefield Mall, taking in the free shows offered periodically. An antique show and sale in the fall is very nice.

Later in the day, drive to Wilson's Creek National Battlefield Park south of the city on Highway 60. Relive history as you follow the line of battle through the park.

A few miles further south is the town of Billings where you can purchase walnut bowls or other wooden gift items.

Then turn east on Highway 14, traveling toward Nixa. Have dinner in one of the restaurants along the way. Then enjoy the country western show presented at the theatre in Nixa. Showtime is 8:30 P.M.

Another full day's relaxing entertainment is to be found to the southeast of the Lebanon area. Travel Highway 5, winding down through the dense, beautiful Ozark forests past Grovespring and Hartsville to Mansfield. The home of Laura Ingalls Wilder, the famous author, is near here.

Turn east here on Highway 60, heading toward Mountain Grove. Here you can enjoy beautiful sightseeing, camping, fishing, golfing, trapshooting, hunting for abundant wild turkey, and delightful picnicking in this remote Ozark range. Take time to sit on the banks and fish for the bass, crappie, and trout that literally fill these waters.

Continue your sightseeing venture to see some of the mills of the area. The closest mill is south of Mountain Grove on Highway 95, then east on Highway AD to EE. Here you can visit the Topaz Mill still in operation.

Stop for a few lazy moments to enjoy this beautiful wonderland. Walk the trails through the forests and watch for deer and small game. Gaze out over the luxurious mountain ranges, watching the shadows dancing on the distant hills.

If you have more time to spend in this area, drive on to Cabool to the east and charter a float on the Big Piney River. The quiet of the river, the magnificence of the huge limestone cliffs, and the cool green of the surrounding foliage offer you unsurpassed relaxation.

Return from your day's tour along Highway 60 west past

Mansfield. Take Highway 5 further south to Ava. Drive the beautiful ridges of the area or take one of the tours offered during the fall months.

Load your camera and stop for a few moments to view the picturesque monastery hidden away in the hills.

For even more beautiful sightseeing, drive Highway 14 east to Highway 125. Turn north on 125, bypassing the Springfield area. Upon reaching Highway 44, turn toward the Lebanon area.

History buffs will want to stop for a tour of the Civil War National Cemetery near Springfield. Turn off Highway 125 onto Highway 60 west, which will carry you to the cemetery.

Pack up your fishing gear and head west of Lebanon along Highway 32 for another fun-filled day in the Stockton Lake area.

You will pass over the Niangua River and the Pomme de Terre River, both excellent bass fishing sites to use another day.

As you travel along, stop at some of the roadside stands or shops for a jug of apple cider or Ozark-made candy such as pralines, clusters, or fudge. A jar of honey also makes an excellent souvenir of your visit to these beautiful Ozark Mountains.

Slow down in Bolivar to view the statue of Simon Bolivar, the famed South American general.

A few miles farther west, follow Highway 245, which drops down south, rolling through the hills and crossing over Lake Stockton. Then turn onto Highway 215 west for still more magnificent scenery as you enter Stockton State Park.

Take your choice of pleasures for the afternoon. Rent a pontoon boat, a houseboat, or a sailboat for drifting along on the clear blue waters of the lake. Or rent a ski boat for an afternoon full of action.

Drop your hook into the water, troll, or cast for elusive

Chamber of Commerce Office (Lebanon, Missouri)

Laura Ingalls Wilder home

northern pike, which abound in these sky blue waters. Winter fishing is also excellent here.

Plan another treat for late afternoon as you board the cruise ship for more sightseeing in this beautiful Ozark arena. The ship operates two cruises a day from May to October.

Return to Highway 215 and continue west across the mile-long bridge that spans the lake. Then follow Highway 39 the short distance into the town of Stockton. Here you may wish to browse through the small shops. Search for items made from native black walnuts. Visit the local walnut products company and take a tour during the walnut season. A walnut and cheese festival is held during the season. Check locally for exact dates.

As you leave the Stockton area on Highway 32, stop to see the dam, located adjacent to the highway. Then follow Highway 32 east, back through the rolling hills and ridges that carry you to the Lebanon area.

If you still have not had your fill of Ozark Mountain lake fishing, take Highway 64 west past Bennett Springs State Park to the Pomme de Terre State Park. Here you will find sandy beaches and clear waters.

Plan to swim and then lunch in the floating restaurant before trying your luck in these bass-laden waters. A Muskie Bass fishing tournament is held during the month of October. Cash prizes draw many top fishermen. Watch as they cast for the largemouth bass, white bass, crappie, bream, and the prized Muskellunge.

If you have time, arrange for a float down the waters of the Pomme de Terre River for more fishing.

TOUR 7

Eminence–Big Spring Area

For true peace, tranquility, and relaxation, plan to visit the Big Spring Country of the Missouri Ozarks. Deep in the backwoods of the magnificent hills, you can hear the gurgling of spring-fed rivers, the splash of fish hooked on your line, and gentle breezes stirring through the tree tops high above.

Nestled among the hills, the area around Eminence, Missouri, offers unsurpassed scenery, hunting, fishing, swimming, picnicking, and very few commercial attractions. Make your reservations early as there are only a few motels and hotels in the area. Campers will find several private campgrounds and a national park campground.

Eminence is located at the junction of Highways 19 and 106 and is an ideal spot for booking a float trip on either Jacks Fork or the Current River. Also make float arrangements early, as many visitors come to explore the waters of the Ozark National Scenic Riverways.

Make a trip up to the top of the fire tower station in Eminence to view the marvelous beauty of the surrounding Ozark hills. Then pack a picnic lunch, grab your fishing gear, take your swimming togs, and head for a day-long exploration of this scenic area. Travel first to the east of Eminence on Highway 106.

Approximately twelve miles away is the Powder Mill Ferry, a beautiful serene attraction surrounded by lush green forests. Drive onto the ferry, settle back, and enjoy the beauty of the dense rugged hills, beautiful blue skies, and crystal clear spring-fed waters.

Disembark at the U.S. Park Visitor Center, where you can check all information regarding campsites and times for local attractions. The national park campground is located just north of the center.

Secure a guide at the center or ask for directions to hike through the heavily wooded forest to nearby Blue Spring. You will see at first glance why the Indians named the spring for its deep blue color.

As you walk through this countryside, formerly occupied by the Indians, search the ground for artifacts indicating their presence many years ago. You might prefer to ride horseback through the hills of the Ozark Mountains.

Continue east on Highway 106 another few miles to the junction with Missouri Highway B. Turn to the north on Highway B, traversing the backwoods sections of the dense Ozark forests. A few miles to the north is Logan Creek Mine. From this point north, you will probably cross paths with prospectors as they search for minerals in this rich mining country.

Continue farther north to the town of Reynolds, where hunting in season is at its finest. Then turn onto Highway 72 east to the junction with Highway 21. Travel north into Lesterville, following the signs to Johnson's Shut Ins State Park. Here the Black River has created a playground combining rocks and rushing waters, offering you hours of perfect fun.

Spread your picnic lunch in the wooded area and enjoy the atmosphere that only nature can create. Swim or wade in the swirling waters. Sunbathe on the highly piled rocks while drinking in the view of Taum Sauk Mountain in the distance. Then spend a few hours dunking your line in the waters for the smallmouth bass.

To return to the Eminence area, follow Highway 21 south along the Ozark Frontier Trail. Stop to explore the Cardareva Cave where, for a small admission, you may examine some of the magnificence found underground in these fabulous Ozark hills.

At the junction of Highways 21 and 106, turn back west on 106, watching for the wild deer as you travel through the dense forests leading into Eminence. Be sure to enjoy a meal of hillbilly cooking at one of the restaurants in the Eminence area. Then check locally for times of the Current River Opry performances or the square dances that are held during the summer months.

A half day's relaxing pleasure is to be found by taking Highway 106 east, turning north on the access road and proceeding a short distance to the Two Rivers Ferry. A leisurely ride will carry you across the clear cool waters at the junction of Jacks Fork and the Current River.

Set aside another full day to explore the area north of Eminence. A few miles north on Highway 19, you will pass through the beautiful virgin pine that lines the scenic drive. Round Spring Caverns is another popular cave awaiting your exploration.

Nearby Round Spring Park is the site of the magnificent Round Spring, which forms a perfect bowl eighty feet wide and thirty feet high. You will enjoy a few moments of unsurpassed serenity beneath the rocky cliffs.

You might also wish to hike the nature trails to nearby Current River or hike to the nearby Indian graves. Spend your leisurely moments fishing, swimming, boating, or canoeing. You may also camp in the park.

Continuing north on Highway 19, turn onto Highway A and then onto Highway CC for a visit to The Sinks. View this natural bridge formed by the erosion of a solid rock wall. The resulting cave gallery, forming the beautiful Emerald Grotto, is a perfect photographic site.

Return to Highway 19, traveling north past Shannondale. Here you may climb the tower, getting a first-hand view of the fabulous countryside.

As you continue along Highway 19, watch for any bears that might roam the wooded areas bordering the road. Travel on through Gladden, turning west onto Highway K a few miles farther north. Follow Highway K to its junction with Highway E. Then proceed on Highway E to Montauk State Park. Spread a picnic lunch or dine in the lodge on the park grounds. Then tour the rainbow trout hatchery, which keeps the stream stocked for unsurpassed trout fishing. Visit the fabulous Seven Springs and then hike some of the nature trails. See the Montauk Mill grind meal. Then set aside some time to wade into the cold, clear waters angling for that fighting rainbow trout.

Retrace your path, turning to the south at the junction with Highway K. Follow K to its junction with KK at the beautiful Current River. Turn east onto Highway KK. It will then merge with Highway J. Follow the signs, turning south on the access road to see Cave Spring. Farther along on Highway J is the spectacular Devil's Well, a particularly interesting natural formation. Two other nearby attractions are the Welch Spring and Pulltite Spring, both producing millions of gallons of water per day. You should make arrangements for a float along the swift waters of Current River in order to view the two.

Bring along your fishing gear, swimming accessories, and walking shoes when you explore the area to the west of Eminence. Travel Highway 106, crossing Jacks Fork River into Alley Spring Park. Alley Spring flows almost 700 million gallons of water daily. And you will most certainly wish to purchase a bag of the meal which is ground here at the Old Red Mill.

Browse through the museum which depicts authentic Ozark culture. Then tour the cave, swim, or simply walk the nature trails which traverse the countryside.

Set aside a few hours for snagging bass in this scenic stream. Then you might roller skate at the local rink, or go horseback riding along the beautiful trails.

Continuing your tour, travel along Highway 106 past The Sunk Lands, one of the most remote and wild areas of these Ozarks. Access is only by jeep, horseback, or hiking, and the services of a guide are required.

Turn north onto Highway K for a scenic drive along the "Devil's Backbone" overlooking the Current River and the breathtaking valley. The Akers Ferry across the river is a perfect way to end a perfect day.

For an unsurpassed view of the Ozarks, take a canoe float downstream from Akers. Of course you may also fish for those hungry bass, trout, jack salmon, or goggle-eye as you float lazily along.

For a half-day adventure, travel west on Highway 106 to Summersville. Climb the fire tower for another marvelous view of the Ozark hills. Take Highway 17, winding down and around through the beautiful forests to Mountain View. Here you will want to spend some time browsing through the glass museum.

Return to the Eminence Area via Highway 60 east, passing through Birch Tree and Bartlett. Take Highway E as it leads north and winds through the back country into Eminence.

A full day of fun awaits you east on Highway 106 to Highway H. Follow H to its junction with Highway HH, which leads you to Rocky Falls. This beautiful attraction is worth the few extra miles, as well as your time.

Return to Highway H, watching for wild game as you pass through the 15,000-acre wild turkey refuge to the town of Winona. Turn east here onto Highway 60, driving through the lush green forests of the Mark Twain National Forest to the town of Van Buren, located on the banks of the Current River. Turn south onto Highway 103, entering Big Springs Park.

Here you will see the world's largest spring, with a flow of one billion gallons per day. Have lunch here at the lodge. Then go for a swim or ride horseback along the scenic trails. Fish or float on the scenic river. Or rent a boat for an afternoon of pleasure on the beautiful waters.

Return to the town of Van Buren for a visit to the Indian museum. Take a stroll through to see the various artifacts of this area.

Travel Highway 60 a few miles east to its junction with Highway 21 north. Enjoy the scenic drive through the magnificent hill country to Highway 106, where you then turn west towards Eminence.

Another area worth your exploration time is south of Eminence. Pack up your fishing gear, because the hungry fish of the Eleven Point River await the plop of your line.

Travel south along Highway 19 through Winona to the river site, where you may rent gear for a day of unsurpassed fishing pleasure.

Wind down through the forests below Winona, taking the access road a few miles to Falling Spring and Mill, another beautiful area in this remote section of the Ozarks.

A few miles further south of Eleven Point River is the town of Greer. The nearby Greer Spring and Mill is well worth your half mile hike through the rustic woods.

Continue past Greer to the junction with Highway 160 at Alton. Then take Highway 160 west a few miles to Highway 99. Here you will turn back north, passing across the Eleven Point River once again.

A few miles further north is an access road leading to Fisher Pond and Old Mines. Venture through the old mines and then return to Highway 99. Continue your trip back to the Eminence area, passing through Birch Tree and Bartlett, joining Highway E.

TOUR 8

Twin Lakes Area

Be it fishing, hunting, boating, water skiing, camping, free floating, canoeing, scuba diving, spelunking, exploring, hiking, local browsing, sightseeing, or just plain loafing, you are certain to find your preference in the Twin Lakes Area of the Ozarks.

Bull Shoals Lake and Lake Norfork offer the ultimate in vacation opportunities. Add to this list the pure simple joys found on Crooked Creek, the cool crispness of the singing White River, and the tremendous, exhilarating beauty of the free flowing Buffalo River wilderness. And you still have only a partial description of yet another nook of this paradise called the Ozarks.

Mountain Home, Arkansas makes an ideal headquarters while visiting in this area. Nestled between the equally beautiful, yet excitingly different lakes, Mountain Home is easily reached at the junction of U.S. Highway 62 and Arkansas Highway 5. An information center located at the junction can provide any and all information desired.

Reservations are an absolute must during peak seasons although the rolling hills abound with modern lodges, resorts, motels, and camping areas. Most of the resorts furnish boats equipped for both fishing and water skiing. Expert guide service is available throughout the area and is a requirement for some of the more remote spots.

You will want to take full advantage of every moment of your visit here. Quickly acquaint yourself with the enormous beauty of the area by taking an inexpensive, lectured sightseeing coach tour, which features panoramic views of both of the beautiful Ozark twin lakes.

Then plan to spend several hours browsing through the Arts & Crafts Association's local shops for a look at authentic handcrafted Arkansas Ozark items. Perhaps an original hand-carved miniature wild bird or a life sized mountaineer fashioned from the local hardwoods will catch your eye. Either will bear the mark of a nationally famous Ozark craftsman. Equally famous are the original button mosaics displayed in the shops.

Set aside one day to explore the area west of Mountain Home. Some of the highways are designated part of the Ozark Frontier Trail and are dotted with numerous interesting historical markers.

Highway 5 meanders six miles northeast to Midway, where it then joins Highway 178 for a beautiful seven-mile drive to the little mountain hamlet of Lakeview. As its name implies, Lakeview offers your first gorgeous view of the beautiful Bull Shoals Lake.

A unique stop is the Whereaway Gift Shop for a look at the most unusual collection of buttons from all over the world. Chief Crazy Horse and other original button mosaics are on display for your browsing pleasure. Next door is the fabulous wood carving collection of the Penrod Museum. Admission is free. For rock hounds, polished samples of some of the stones which abound in the Ozarks are found at the nearby Rock Shop.

Lakeview is also a hunter's paradise, offering both winter and summer hunting for game such as deer, turkey, quail, squirrel, and duck. You may fish for walleye, crappie, channel cat, bass, or trout. There are no closed fishing seasons or mosquitoes in this area of the Ozarks to hamper the fun. Night fishing by lantern light for the fighting trout is fascinating.

Leaving Lakeview, continue on Highway 178 across Bull Shoals Dam. Above the dam, you can see the beautiful Bull Shoals Lake, home of the lunker largemouth bass. Ten to twelve pounders are not at all unusual for this lake, which also boasts smallmouth, Kentucky (spotted) bass, white bass, and drum.

Below the dam, the beautiful White River snakes its way down through the mountains and gorges of the Ozarks. A leisurely float trip in a johnboat casting for the rainbow or German trout which fill these waters is the fisherman's ultimate desire, especially when he can end his day by devouring a delicious trout dinner from his catch. The trout reach gigantic size on the White: rainbow are up to 14¼ pounds and German Brown up to 28 pounds on spinning tackle.

Around the bend from the dam is Bull Shoals State Park. Stop here to walk down to the water's edge. The park is equipped with a lodge and both lake and riverside campsites. A trout dock offers guide and float service.

Available here also are diving stations and guides for scuba enthusiasts. Most divers are amazed to see how clear the water is on Bull Shoals at depths to 150 feet.

The dam area is an excellent put-in point for a float trip of a day, overnight, or even several days. For a short float, you can put in here. Prior arrangements will be made to take out at Cotter, eighteen miles to the south. Bring along a box lunch for a picnic on a sand bar. When you reach Cotter, you will be driven back to your original starting point.

For a longer trip, you might want to float to Matney Campground, a remote area of the Ozark Forest accessible only by water or hiking trail. The ever changing scenic bluffs of sparkling limestone lining the White make gorgeous photographic or artist models. You may even be treated to an impromptu exhibition of intricate maneuvers by expert skiers as you drift lazily along. At the campground, you can hike through unspoiled lush hardwood forests.

Continuing on your tour of the area, drive immediately past the park and turn into Mountain Village, 1890. To understand how the mountain people lived in the past, take a guided tour to see them presently living in fully restored dwellings, complete with "dog trots" down the middle and quilting frames hung from the ceilings.

Visit their general store, one-room school house, and blacksmith and coffin shops. Go with them to the village waterpump. Then hurry to the little white church when summoned by the bell, sounded with a swinging rope. Sit in the Amen Corner. Stay for dinner on the grounds while the children enjoy free donkey and pony rides.

Afterwards, tour the Bull Shoals Caverns, where all known cave formations exist. Get a close view of those giant trout in the underground stream. Your guided tour will be relaxing in the fifty-nine degree temperature with no stairs to climb. Then you will want to take the elevator twenty stories up to Top O'The Ozarks Tower for a view of more than a million acres of breathtaking Ozark hill country.

Continue on Highway 178 to the tiny mountain town of Flippin where Highway 178 crosses Highway 62 for the return to Mountain Home.

Rock collectors will want to allow time for an excursion in to the sparsely settled Peel Area of Bull Shoals approximately thirty miles from Flippin. To reach Peel, turn west on Highway 62 to Yellville. Take Highway 14 north to its junction with Highway 125. Follow Highway 125 into the Peel Area. After a time of rock collecting, ride the free ferry across Bull Shoals Lake for a leisurely bit of sightseeing in the Missouri Ozarks. This bit of Bull Shoals Lake also abounds with largemouth bass, crappie, jack salmon, white bass, and the famous White River catfish.

For more information regarding local hunting and field trips, contact the Rockhound Earth Science Club. Monthly meetings are open to all visitors every second Tuesday at 8:00 P.M. in the Mountain Home Community Center.

Returning to Highway 62 at Flippin, sit back and enjoy the rustic beauty of the Ozarks as you pass over the White River at Cotter. The homes of Cotter, built like stair steps up the steep bluff from the river, are typical of those found elsewhere in the Ozarks. Quiet streets, flower-filled yards, and small town atmosphere prevails.

Plan to enjoy the Rainbow Valley Hillbilly performances presented every Tuesday and Friday night at 8:00 P.M. during the summer months. Small admission is charged. Also for those interested, the Arkansas Gun Club east of Cotter is open April 1 to September 1 every Sunday afternoon and Wednesday night.

Slow down for a look at Gassville, another small Ozark town, as you wind your way back to Mountain Home.

You will want to spend at least one day and evening exploring the area to the east of Mountain Home. Taking Highway 5 south, drive 14 miles to the little town of Norfork, where the White and Norfork rivers join. Here you may tour the oldest Arkansas log cabin still standing. Built six years after the Louisiana Purchase, Wolf House was once the center of North Arkansas social, political, religious, business, and cultural life. Among its famous guests were Davy Crockett and Sam Houston. The house contains over 400 relics and pieces of period furniture for your leisurely inspection at a modest admission cost.

Returning to Highway 5, follow the signs to the country's largest federal trout hatchery, located just below Norfork Dam. Here you will be treated to a most fascinating guided

Wolf House (Norfolk, Arkansas)

Buffalo River, Bull Shoals Area

tour any day of the year. You will follow the growth of the rainbow trout through each successive stage from egg to release size. This "fish factory" produces 1½ million trout per year to provide sport for anglers who come to fish these cold Arkansas waters.

Nearby Norfork Dam forms the crystal clear Lake Norfork with the North Fork River angling off below the dam. Spinning, bait, and fly casting are recommended for the tackle busting trout in North Fork River. Float trips may be arranged here also.

Norfork Lake enjoys a world wide reputation for lunker bass, with the largemouth weighing up to twelve pounds. September though May is the ideal time for catching the deep black bass. Pontoon night fishing for bass and crappie is excellent during the summer months.

The wooded hills surrounding Lake Norfork offer the best in season hunting for whitetail deer, rabbits, ducks, geese, doves, quail, and turkey. Hiking is very popular also; check with the local Corps of Engineers office to assure a safe and interesting expedition.

This lake is perfect for sailing and water skiing. Excellent marinas and accommodations abound. Scuba divers will enjoy exploring the underground caves and bridges covered over when the lake was formed. Lake Norfork is considered one of the best in the nation for this aquatic sport because of its crystal clear calm waters. Game spearfishing is allowed and divers spear scaled rough fish during the daylight hours. Equally interesting is the river diving and spring diving also available in this area. All pertinent information regarding guide services and best diving locations is available from the local scuba shops.

As you travel north on Highway 5 for your return to Mountain Home, you can find a perfect spot for a picnic or campout by following one of the side roads leading into the lake area.

There are many boat docks, easy access to the water, and good roads to the water's edge.

Returning to Mountain Home, take Ozark Frontier Trail Highway 62 ten miles east to the free ferry that crosses Lake Norfork. This will provide an opportunity for some spectacular sightseeing as you drift slowly across the cold, clear shimmering waters. Highway 101 to the north will take you to more fishing areas, campsites, parks, and docks.

Continuing on Highway 62 twenty-six miles further east will bring you to the tiny community of Salem, deep in the Ozark hills. Each Saturday night, you can clap your hands and tap your feet as you are treated to an old-fashioned hill country musical. The mountain folk of Arkansas and Missouri come together at 7:30 P.M. to ply your ears for three hours with the music that is a natural way of life for them. There is no admission charge.

Salem offers a spectacular view from its fire tower located in Pilot Point, an important Civil War landmark.

Another outing in the area east of Mountain Home will take you twenty miles past Salem on scenic Highway 9 to the town of Mammoth Spring. The Mammoth Spring State Park offers an authentically restored train depot, one of the first on the Frisco Line, for your browsing enjoyment. A federal fish hatchery nearby features an aquarium which contains all the species of fish that inhabit this area.

The main attraction, however, is the spectacular Mammoth Spring, one of the world's largest, which gushes forth 200 million gallons of water per day, forming an eighteen acre lake and the beautiful, serene Spring River. As an angler, you will have the perfect opportunity for fly fishing while wading in the cold waters of the river's first three miles. The trout are smaller, only three to six pounds, but they bite well on corn, cheese, salmon eggs, or red worms.

Farther along, the river picks up speed as it washes over the shoals. This provides you with the opportunity to "shoot the rapids" in a canoe. At least one spill is to be expected on your one-way roller coaster ride downriver to the Many Islands Camp Grounds, where you can fish for the trout using Rooster Tail, Mepps, and similar small spinners. After your limit is assured, settle back in the canoe, forget everything, and enjoy the complete solitude and scenic beauty as you relax under the towering bluffs of the majestic Ozark Mountains.

Later in the day, you will want to travel the sixteen miles on Highway 63 south to Hardy. The public beach here is a favorite swimming hole.

Be sure to take time to travel four miles east on Highway 64 to the Sugar Creek Craft Shop, where you are assured authentic Ozark crafts. You can enjoy the tales of folklore and folk knowledge that the shopkeeper will dispense while you search for that just right souvenir. An apple-head or wishbone doll would be a good selection. Or perhaps a wooden toy fashioned by hand, or handmade dulcimers may be more to your liking. You will also be able to find a pickin' bow along with directions on just how to play it. The shop is open all year, except January through March.

Early in the evening, follow U.S. 167 three miles southeast of Hardy to the isolated and wooded Arkansas Traveller Folk Theatre. Arrive in time to enjoy the squatter's dinner of beans and ham hock, Ozark salt pork, greens, hill potatoes, corn bread, slaw, dessert, and sassafras tea, served from 6:00 to 8:30 P.M. Then join in the singing and foot tapping that accompanies this famous Ozark folk tale. Designed for the whole family's enjoyment, the children will especially enjoy the live animals in the show. Shows are presented on Tuesday, Thursday, and Saturday nights during the summer months. Gate admission is quite reasonable and the meal is optional.

Leaving the Hardy area, follow Highway 63 south to the junction at Ash Flat. Turn here on Highway 62 west for a return scenic route through Salem and back to Mountain Home.

This area of the Ozark hills is a haven for large retirement villages and resort developments. Some feature beautiful lodges and spas for your visiting enjoyment. Most offer campgrounds, horseback riding, golf, rodeos, tennis, and all types of family entertainment.

Horseshoe Bend, located six miles south on Arkansas 289 has an annual Ridiculous Day. A Frontier Village and Museum, plus a Wildlife Park and a Music Mountain Theatre with announced performances, make another worthwhile side trip.

The next area of the Ozarks to explore is north of Mountain Home. This portion of the Ozarks is equally as interesting, although entirely different from those previously visited.

Follow Ozark Frontier Trail Highway 5 again to Midway where it then turns north for the trip into the Missouri Ozarks. Continue through the town of Three Brothers while you enjoy the ever changing beauty of the Ozark hills.

In spring the dogwoods splash the countryside with their display of white and pink. Summer brings lush green intermingled with bouncing shadows. Then fall with its famous Flaming Revue flashes crimson, yellow, and gold leaves across the mountains and down through the hollers until winter polka dots the landscape with evergreens and bare, stark upshot limbs.

The area west of Highway 5 contains many private resorts on Bull Shoals Lake. There are no public access areas to the lake at this point.

Crossing into Missouri, continue on Highway 5 to its junction with U.S. Highway 160, which will carry you into the town of Gainesville. The Annual Hootin' an' Hollarin' Festival is held each year during the first week of October. For three days, everyone turns out for picking and singing, terrapin races, singing in brush arbors, stilt races, and dinner on the grounds. There are also nail driving contests for the women, a parade, and husband, cow, and hog calling contests plus square dancing each evening.

The area around Gainesville abounds with interesting sights. More than 240 Indian mounds have been counted. Remains of ancient campsites are common along the valley streams.

Public recreation areas are quite numerous with fishing, water sports, float trips, and hunting quite popular. You might enjoy taking part in the Caney Refuge primitive weapons hunting season during the Fall.

Referred to as Mill Country because of its many water driven grain mills, this area features several tours of these mills.

The first mill to tour, Rockbridge Mill, is now a feature of a trout fishing resort. Travel two miles east on U.S. 160 from Gainesville to State Highway 181, then left six miles to Route N. Turn left 9½ miles to Rockbridge Mill. Milling was done here by hand before the time of the Civil War.

The Zanoni Mill, two miles further east on Highway 181, features an overshot wheel which was once turned by a spring. Check your camera for film because Hodgson Mill, next on the tour, is a perfect photographic model. Travel six miles further east on Highway 181 to see the mill still in operation.

You may deviate here from the mill tour in order to take full advantage of the beauty of the Blue Springs area of Mark Twain National Forest. Travel seven miles on Highway 181 to Route F102, which will lead you to the Blue Springs area.

After a short hike through the magnificent countryside, return to Highway 181, traveling three miles to Route H. Turn south here to the junction with Route PP. Follow the signs to Dawt Mill, crossing the upper section of the North

Fork River. Stop here to take a short float trip on the river. The Dawt Mill dam is a special treat of the trip. Meal is still ground occasionally at this mill.

Continue south on Route PP until reaching Highway 160. Turn east and travel on Highway 160 to the junction with 101. Take 101 down the scenic drive through the Ozarks surrounding Lake Norfork. Board the free ferry at the lake for a lazy ride across the smooth waters before driving the last ten miles into Mountain Home.

A trip into the rugged, scenic country to the southwest of Mountain Home is next on the agenda. Follow Highway 62 to the town of Yellville twenty-two miles away.

Try to be on hand for the annual Turkey Trot, held in October each year. For two days, fun and merrymaking are the order of the day. A carnival is held with games, exhibits, arts and crafts. There is an annual talent show hosted by a professional entertainer. A parade, dance, and the National Wild Turkey Calling Contest bring many visitors to the area. You will want to stay for the sit-down dinner held at the school where you can get all the turkey and cornbread dressing you can eat for a nominal fee.

While in Yellville, you might wish to make arrangements to float one of the area's best fish-producing streams, Crooked Creek. A guide is necessary in order to maneuver your boat through the twisting, turning, tumbling waters to the fishing holes where the large bass await your line. The remoteness of this area is also conducive to archery and trapshooting.

Before leaving the town of Yellville, stop in the county square for some homemade pastries or sandwiches to take along. Then turn south along Highway 14 towards the beautiful, breathtaking Buffalo National River Area.

Four miles below Yellville is the city-owned Artesian Well with the Rainbow Springs Trout Farm nearby. The tiny town of Ralph makes its appearance also.

Hodgson Mill

Two miles farther, branch off on an unpaved road leading to the ghost town of Rush, where you can treasure hunt in the old buildings and visit one of the deserted zinc mines that honeycomb these hills. If you plan to float the Buffalo, you can enjoy this treat as part of your float trip.

Turn off the highway to visit the Shawnee Cave eight miles south of Yellville. The cave has been the home of cavemen, bluff dwellers, and Indians. It is well lighted and boasts fine crystal formations, crude stone artifacts, and arrow collections. Tours are held every thirty minutes.

A little farther south, turn onto Highway 268 leading to the Buffalo National River Recreational Point. Campsites, rental cabins, dining room, picnic areas, rental canoes, and guide service are all available to supply you with all the necessities to swim, hike, explore, float, and enjoy.

Hike the nature trails to the Rock House and Bat Cave. Explore the hidden springs and other caves in the area. Check with the National Park Service regarding nature exhibits, nature trails, and other interesting points.

To experience the true essence of this Ozark country, you must float the magnificent Buffalo River. Challenge the gushing white water chutes leading into the wilderness, populated only by towering limestone bluffs and rich unspoiled forests. Watch the bluffs fall away and the gushing rapids become cold clear pools full of lurking bass and trout. Check with the concessionaire in the park to make arrangements for one of these floats. A one day trip will take you to the old mining town of Rush. Or you can just move leisurely downriver to any designated take-out point. Whatever you choose, a shuttle service is available to return you to your starting point.

If you plan to stay in this area of the Ozarks, reservations are absolutely necessary; the Buffalo is quite popular.

Try one more adventure as you wend your way back to Yellville. Turn off at Shawnee Cave again and follow the road

Rockbridge Mill

past the cave to Bruno. From here a scenic skyline drive will lead you along Highway 235 back to the town of Yellville. All of the drives in this area are scenic, but this one is truly spectacular.

TOUR 9

Mountain View Area

Travel back in time to the days of the original pioneers of the Ozark Mountains with a visit to the Ozark Folk Center located at Mountain View, Arkansas. Here you can see and talk with some of the direct descendants of those early mountain settlers as they demonstrate daily their folk crafts.

This cradle of Ozark Mountain culture can be reached via Arkansas Highways 5, 9, 14, or 66, all of which come tumbling down out of the gorgeous rolling hills surrounding the center. Facilities at the center are excellent. Reservations are an absolute must if you plan to stay in the lodge located on the center grounds. Early reservations are advisable for any of the motels, hotels, lodges, or campgrounds in the surrounding hills. The Folk Center opens its annual season with an old-time Ozark Folk Festival held on consecutive weekends during the month of April.

Any season is a perfect one for a visit to these hills, but a springtime visit is a particular delight with the blooming dogwoods, sarvis berry, wild plum, and redbuds filling the mountainsides with fabulous pastels.

From the moment you first step on the center grounds, you are drawn into the traditional culture of this isolated land. You must first explore the pioneer farm and village structures for a look at the ways and means of yesteryear. These replicas have been erected on the center grounds by the mountaineers themselves.

Stop for a moment to tap your foot and clap your hands to the impromptu jug and string band as it strikes up "Barbara Allen" or "Knoxville Girl." A nearby mountaineer will probably break into an old-time jig.

Next make your way to the various craft displays exhibited for your interest and enjoyment. No merchandise is sold in the display areas. If you wish to purchase a souvenir later, you may do so at one of the centrally located shops. But for now, simply take your time visiting with the craftsmen and watching as they show you how it was originally done in the Ozark hills.

Take time to ask questions or swap tales with the craftsmen. You may even join a folklore class so that you, too, might learn a bit about the remarkable heritage of the Ozark Mountains.

Beginning May 1, a continuous folk festival is held at the center every day during the summer months. You will see the mountain men producing hand-crafted knives, powder horns, tanned hides, or handmade rifles. Follow the ring of the anvil to observe the old-time blacksmith at work. Women will show you how candles were made, quilting done, or how foods were canned and preserved many years ago.

Stop for lunch in the spacious restaurant on the grounds. Take your choice of such delicacies as Arkansas fried chicken, country-smoked ham with red-eye gravy, or freshly caught White River catfish. Add a helping of poke salad greens, black-eyed peas, or yams. Spread freshly churned butter on the buttermilk biscuits or cornbread and dig into a real old-time country feast.

After such a hearty lunch, you will want to spend more time touring the various craft displays. Watch as the wood carver whittles his wares. You will be fascinated by the potter's handwork. Help weave a basket or a handmade broom. Participate in the old-time soapmaking. See the spinners and weavers as they perform their old-time crafts and watch as the women fashion the individual apple dolls. Stop by to see the primitive furniture being made today just as it was generations ago.

As your day nears an end, make plans to attend the folk music concert held each night except Sunday in the auditorium on the center grounds. For a small fee, you can hear the plaintive and the playful tunes that have echoed through these hills and hollers for generations. Dance a jig with the native Ozarkians to music by banjos, guitars, "pickin' bows" and mountain dulcimers. Also on Sundays you can join in the old-time gospel sing held at 2:00 in the auditorium. This living museum of the mountains closes its season with a Family Harvest Festival during the month of October. During this time, you can join with the pioneer family as it prepares for the long wintry months ahead.

One week of the festival honors the fathers of these mountains. Special features include a regional muzzle-loading rifle contest in preparation for the muzzle-loading deer hunting season beginning in mid-October. Enjoy a goat and turkey roast during that weekend with the contestants all dressed in full regalia of their sport.

Whittling, checkers, and tall tale contests draw many spectators. You will enjoy the exhibits of old-time fishing gear and firearms. You can also see knives, arrowheads, shingles, and rails demonstrated. An old-time dress revue is a feature of Mother's Week. Sentimental ballads are sung to the accompaniment of the dulcimer and autoharp. Square dancing is performed on both the indoor and outdoor stages of the auditorium.

A mountain recipe contest is one of the highlights of the many food demonstrations. You will want to sample some of the wares of these talented mountain women. You may even join the mothers as they prepare their quilts for the cold winter nights ahead.

Children's Week features dramatizations of Ozark folklore and pioneer folk music. See the award-winning demonstrations of clay, marbles, horseshoes, tomwalking, and jump rope. Join in the "play party" games, crafts, dances, and songs presented by the mountain children.

As the whole family prepares for the cold months ahead, there is much food preparation, including canning, harvesting, and storage. See how the mountain families really existed in this remote region generations ago. A mule-drawn sorghum mill operates while preparations go on for such staples as hominy, soap, jams, pickles, apple butter, and the smoking of old-time country hams.

Join in the family storytelling and the ballad sings. Then take time out to walk the rugged trails and to smell autumn in the air. The season is climaxed with a fiddler's contest, which draws musicians from several states. The resulting jamboree is an evening you will long remember.

As you leave the center, be sure to stop at the Dulcimer Shoppe and Stone County Pottery Shop for a last bit of browsing before turning north onto Highways 9, 5, and 14 for another magnificent treat. The Sylamore Creek Craft Shop on the highway also features authentic merchandise.

Travel a short five miles north where you will enter the Sylamore District of the Ozark National Forest. Slow down to a snail's pace, as you are about to be treated to some of the most beautiful scenery in the country. You may also hunt, fish, hike, ride, sightsee, birdwatch, pick berries, collect rocks, camp, boat, or picnic to your heart's content during your sojourn in the forest.

Upon reaching the village of Allison, turn west to follow Highway 14, which will lead you to Blanchard Springs Caverns. Named for Col. John Blanchard, the man who originally homesteaded this land in the early nineteenth century, Blanchard Springs Caverns is located on Highway 14, fifteen

Ozark quilting and spinning, Ozark Folk Center (Mountain View, Arkansas)

Mountain musician

miles northwest of Mountain View, Arkansas. The caverns have been compared in beauty and size to the Carlsbad Caverns in New Mexico and Mammoth Cave in Kentucky.

But Colonel Blanchard never dreamed there were miles and miles of beautiful formations beneath his land. For to him, there was only a mysterious hole in one side of the mountain and a free flowing spring in the other side of the hill. He built a grist mill on the spring and made his livelihood grinding corn for his neighbors.

Then in the 1930s, long after Colonel Blanchard's days, some of the local residents began to suspect that there might be a connection between the deep dark hole in the side of the mountain and the spring a half mile away. So they decided to conduct an experiment. They dropped cornstalks into the dark hole, heard them splash in water deep down in the mountain, and then watched to see if they emerged from the spring.

You can only imagine their surprise when their cornstalks did emerge—twenty-four hours later. They could only guess what lay beneath the Ozark hills that caused their cornstalks to take twenty-four hours to travel less than one-half mile.

No one dared to enter the cave by the dark hole though, as it dropped straight down more than seventy feet. And the spring entrance was much too small for man to navigate. So the caverns held their dark secrets for additional decades.

Eventually the land became part of the Ozark National Forest and in 1960, spelunkers became interested in the cave. After several amateur explorations, the U.S. Forest Service sent scuba divers into the caverns to explore the mysterious watercourse all the way from the natural entrance in the hole in the side of the mountain to the springs entrance. The divers reported remarkable beauty in cave formations and beautiful waterfalls.

Since the natural entrance was unusable for visitors, the

Forest Service has installed an elevator that descends 216 feet deep into the earth. It opens into the gigantic Cathedral Room, which is large enough to hold more than three football fields.

The Dripstone Trail, opened to tourists in the summer of 1973, is fully lighted and planned for safety. A tour, directed by a guide, covers almost a mile in an hour and a half. Admission is $2 for adults and $1 for children.

Along and beside the Dripstone Trail are formations of every kind. Soda straws, massive flowstones, and stalagmites are at every turn. The Coral Room features a coral pond with fragile lacy patterns, draperies, and popcorn crystal. A natural bridge of gravel leads to huge piles of cavern ceiling that fell ages ago.

Other tours, including a boat ride along the stream leading to one of the cavern's most spectacular formations, the Giant Flowstone, which is 150 feet long and 30 feet high and is the largest known deposit of calcium carbonate in the world, will be opened soon.

Above ground accommodations include swimming, fishing, picnicking, camping, hiking, horseback riding, nature walks, and scenic drives. Day and evening lecture programs are scheduled by the Forest Service in the outdoor amphitheater located beneath a towering Ozark Mountain bluff.

Tours of the caverns begin every twenty minutes with the first at 9:20 A.M.

When you emerge from the caverns, take the rustic, winding bridge to beautiful Blanchard Springs, where the waters gush forth from deep inside the caverns. The old mill once served the pioneers of this area and can still be seen downstream from the springs. You may wish to hike one of the nature trails through the lush forests above the caverns. Stop for a picnic beneath a towering Ozark bluff.

Next drive into the nearby Gunner Pool Area, which is

three miles northeast on a gravelled forest service road. Here you can wiggle your toes in the clear stream, see the fish jump in the small lake, hike the picturesque bluffs, or swim or hunt in season.

For a sightseeing tour of the area, drive on past Blanchard Springs Caverns to Fifty-Six, a region virtually untouched by civilization. The scenery here is truly breaktaking. Take your time driving the steep, crooked highways that wind down, up, around, and through these magnificent hills.

This is the true Ozark land, where the pioneer had to dig his way through the rocks in order to raise enough food for his family. The porch columns on hillbilly shacks are still fashioned from saplings and plowed fields look like dry gray ashes splattered with stones. The meadows of golden sage, green grass, and dormant fields roll and tumble across the land until at last they crash into the mountains, which reverberate range after range as far as the eyes can see.

Enjoy more spectacular Ozark scenery as you circle around the ridges past Big Flat into the crossroads village of Harriet.

You will note the canoe liveries on Highway 14 north, for in the Buffalo National Scenic River area, floating the Buffalo is a favorite pastime.

To continue your scenic drive, follow Highway 27 west. Note the vertically plowed rocky ridges that denote Flintrock Strawberry country. The vertical plowing keeps the sand off these luscious berries as they ripen. As you pass through Lone Pine and Morning Star, you will notice stands offering these berries for sale. At the bottom of the ridge is the market center of the strawberry country, Marshall. Picking time in spring brings in all the natives for the Strawberry Festival. Be sure to try a portion of the local strawberry shortcake any time of the year.

Highway 65 south, cut from solid rock, will lead you to Leslie, located on the Little Red River. You can camp here for a day of fishing or visit one of the dude ranches located in this area of the Ozark hills. Turn south at Leslie onto Highway 66. Once again you are in the deeper, more remote section of the Ozarks as you ramble past Oxley, through Alco, and into Timbo. The home of Jimmy Driftwood, nationally known folk singer, is here in Timbo. The last thirteen miles of your scenic drive along Highway 66 will take you back into Mountain View.

Allow a full day to explore some of the area to the north and east of Mountain View. Follow Highway 5 north as it winds through the beautiful Ozark National Forest, leading to the tiny river port of Calico Rock. Named when steamboats traveled up the river, Calico Rock is perched high on a bluff overlooking the marvelous White River.

Cross over the river for a leisurely stop in this quaint, colorful gem of the Ozarks. Summer fun begins here with a rodeo in June, followed by a trout fishing derby, continuing into July.

Walk the town square, stopping to browse through the small shops. Then leave Calico Rock and continue north for a few miles, turning to the east on Highway 56. Travel thirteen miles to the tiny town of Brockwell. Here you will turn south onto Highway 9 leading to the mountain village of Melbourne, where you can see a Saturday night mountain music show.

Continue to travel south on Highway 9 through this sparsely settled region. This is considered one of the most beautiful drives in the Ozark Mountains. A few miles farther south, at a place called Twin Creeks, take a gravel road leading to the old ghost town of Mt. Olive. Explore the area and then take time to fish for those elusive trout in the White River. Return to Highway 9 and then join Highway 5 for the return to Mountain View.

For a unique trip back in time, visit Batesville, a river town of the 1800s. Travel Highway 14 south, turning onto Highway 25, which will then carry you into Batesville. You will enjoy walking through this town where the old homes of another era still stand. During the summer months, there are swimming meets, speedboat regattas, and bathing beauty contests as part of the annual White River Water Carnival. Be sure to stop for a lunch of White River trout or fresh catfish.

Drive northwest of Batesville on Highway 69, stopping to see the Old Spring Mill. You can tour the mill and then stop in the museum to examine artifacts of the 1800s. Then turn onto Highway 58 leading to the town of Guion, an old river port and railroad center of long ago. Rare St. Petersburg sandstone was mined here for shipment to glass factories. Stop at the tavern for a delightful few moments. Then tour the railroad depot, which has been restored in period style. Browse through the antique shop in the freight room and ticket office. Ride the free ferry across this remote section of the White. Then proceed on a gravel road leading you back to Highway 14 and on to Mountain View, or return via Melbourne and Highway 9 south to Sylamore.

If you have more time to spend exploring this area, begin another trip from the town of Marshall. Traveling north on Highway 65 will carry you to some of the most rugged and beautiful of all the Ozark areas. Here on the Buffalo are many waterfalls, canyons, and deteriorated cabins dotting the hills.

Check locally for hiking information. If you wish, set out to hike down one canyon and back up another, although this is not recommended for the armchair traveler.

Those more accustomed to scenic driving can follow Highway 27 down through the rugged country south of Marshall. Be sure your camera is loaded for the scenic snapshots.

Highway 27 joins Highway 16 as you turn back north. Stop at Witts Spring for one of the most beautiful of all sights. Then continue north on Highway 377, an unpaved, but good, road cut through the wilderness. Stop at Snowball for a last look at this basically undeveloped land of the past.

TOUR 10

Harrison Area

Located on U.S. Highway 65 at its junction with Arkansas Highways 7 and 43, Harrison, Arkansas, attracts a great many visitors each year. Reservations are an absolute must during the busy summer months, as many tourists explore the central section of the Ozark Mountains. Stop in at the gallery to see the paintings on display anytime during the weekdays and until 2:00 on Saturdays. The Ozark Country Music Theatre on Highway 65 north may have performances during your visit. Check locally for times and prices. The Annual Blue Grass Music Festival attracts many top artists during the late summer. Join in the fun at the fairgrounds if this coincides with your visit.

Begin your exploration of the surrounding area with a visit to the south of Harrison on Highway 7. Considered one of the most scenic routes in the country, Highway 7 attracts many visitors. Its winding, hairpin, scenic route is perfect for viewing the dogwoods of spring, the beautiful changing colors of fall, and the rich green blanket of summer.

Seven miles south of Harrison is the Bryant Art Museum, located in the former Krooked Kreek School. Admission is nominal and your time will be well spent viewing the exhibits of original paintings by 17th to 20th century world famous artists. Original Ozark paintings are offered for purchase in the adjoining gift shop.

Next stop is for a full day of outlandish fun at one of the "Great Twin Parks in the Ozarks," Dogpatch, U.S.A. located just nine miles south of Harrison. Motels, lodges, private chalets, apartments, and a Campark are available here for your convenience.

Admission to the theme park covers fares on most rides and shows including the Swiss Funicular cable car which zooms you down into the valley of Dogpatch, U.S.A. Turn the children loose to enjoy the animal farm, watch the educated animal shows, or even to catch a rainbow trout in the lake.

Get a whiff of Barney Barnsmell's Skunk-Works and see General Bullmoose's Dark Light Maze and Gravity House. Take a trip on Earthquake McGoon's Brain Rattler. Then enjoy a luscious hand packed ice cream cone while waiting for the West Po'k Chop Speshul to carry you to downtown Dogpatch where arts and crafts shops surround the famous statue of General Cornpone. Watch the native craftsmen at work while you browse. You might even purchase a genuine corn cob pipe just like Mammy Yokum's. Have a larapin' sandwich at a snack shop and then drop in for a show at the Kornvention Hall.

Purchase an inexpensive portion of these Ozark Mountains at the Rock Shop. Then hike the trail leading up the hill to the three authentic Ozark shacks perched precariously overlooking downtown Dogpatch. But watch out for Marryin' Sam or you may find yourself hitched up to Moonbeam McSwine or Hairless Joe.

Enjoy a leisurely two minute tour through the one room shack belonging to Li'l Abner and Daisy Mae. Check your appearance in the jagged mirror hanging in Mammy Yokum's kitchen next door. Then have your picture made with Lonesome Polecat out on the front porch.

Hop on Li'l Abner's Space Rocket for a ride into outer space. Joe Btfsplk's Impendin' Disaster awaits those who survive.

You will want to read the hilarious headstones in the graveyard beside the tiny chapel before reboarding the Swiss Funicular for a ride back up the hill to the shopping area located above Dogpatch.

Dogpatch is open daily during the summer and on weekends in May and September. Hours are 9 to 6. Small children are free and the admission is quite reasonable.

Save your tickets as the admission to nearby Dogpatch Caverns is one-half price for Dogpatch ticket holders. The inside of these beautiful Ozark hills is equally as interesting and entertaining as the outside is.

Shop the mall, swim, or skate. Finish off your day at the Mid-Ozarks Jamboree Theater at 8:30 P.M.

This area of the Ozarks also features horseback riding, hiking, tennis, golf, excellent restaurants, and of course hours and hours of browsing through the interesting shops.

Set aside another day for a spectacular scenic drive further down Highway 7 through the lush, jagged center of this Ozark wonderland. Fifteen miles south of Harrison is Paradise Hill. That delicious odor permeating the mountain air is a smokehouse at work.

A stop for a sandwich of true Ozark smoked meat is an absolute must on a visit here. Take your choice of hickory smoked or sugar cured ham, bacon, pork, or summer sausage. This meat is much in demand and the shop will gladly ship some to your home for later use.

Ask to take a tour of the smokehouse to see how this excellent taste is achieved. After a scrumptious sandwich served up with lots of free coffee, you will want to tour the other shops here at Paradise Hill.

Handmade wooden toys, paintings, jewelry, herbs, leather goods, quilts, needlework, and even traditional musical instruments of the mountains such as dulcimers, are all available here.

You might enjoy a honey sundae while watching a colony of honeybees at work.

Stroll down to Lookout Point to see the spectacular Buffalo National River Monument, a recent sculpture. If you brought your bathing duds, you may even take a quick dip in the local swimming hole here in the Buffalo. Float trips are available from here to view yet another scenic area of the famed Buffalo.

Another five miles south on Highway 7 will bring you to the tiny backhills town of Jasper. Turn here onto Highway 74 west leading into the remote wilderness of the upper Buffalo River Valley.

The popular Diamond Cave, four miles from Jasper, offers two-hour tours leaving every thirty minutes during the daylight hours. Visit the pioneer shack nearby and take a short walk through the scenic, rustic Ozark woods.

Nine more miles of well-traveled gravel road will lead you to one of the best put-in spots of the shallow headwaters of the Buffalo, the low-water bridge across the river near Ponca. The boaters queue up when the water is high for the exciting canoe ride through the tallest bluffs and whitest waters on this beautiful stream.

The old mining town of Ponca will serve as an excellent base for a visit into Lost Valley State Park two miles south. Lost Valley Lodge can provide you with all pertinent information regarding a hike into this beautiful wonderland of rugged wilderness. The park is equipped with picnic areas and water for the outdoorsman as he explores the many caves and cliffs.

Entrance to Lost Valley State Park is gained through a natural cave leading into the breathtaking hidden valley, walled in on three sides by steep limestone bluffs. Hike along the creek beds to beautiful "No Places." Explore Hemmed-In Hollow, a box canyon located along the river. The sheer rock walls 250 feet high will take your breath away with their cascading waterfall. Nearby is the Big Bluff Trail, which leads you along the tops of huge bluffs overlooking the Buffalo River Valley for more spectacular sights. This is not recommended for the inexperienced hiker.

Leaving Ponca, travel along the mountain ranges of Highway 43 leading towards Harrison. Gaither Mountain Park offers yet another spectacular sight with a view of Harrison and Crooked Creek Valley. Hikers will want to travel still farther south of Harrison on Highway 7, turning west on Highway 16 for a visit to the Alum Cove area of the Ozark National Forest. The scenery is unsurpassed and the rugged terrain a challenge.

From Alum Cove, you may travel back into Harrison via Highway 21 north through Boxley near the Buffalo headwaters. From Boxley, travel five miles on unpaved road to Ponca with the same return to Harrison via Highway 43.

For more sightseeing, travel south on Highway 7 as the road swoops, bends, and glides through the beautiful Ozark forests. There are several lookout points where you can stop for a view of the rivers, streams, and waterfalls that spill down the valleys below.

As you climb into the mountains on Highway 7, a stop at Booger Hollow, Arkansas, is an absolute must. With a population of 7, including one coon dog, Booger Hollow's sole purpose is to serve the traveler.

The trading post features local information as its prime asset. You have only to ask and the proprietors will fill you in on local events of interest, sightseeing, fishing, hunting, and camping.

The store also features an antique corner where the local natives display their keepsake heirlooms for sale. Often antique treasures can be found at very reasonable prices.

For a welcome respite, enjoy true hickory-smoked ham at

the local restaurant. Then enjoy the leisurely drive back through the ever-changing wilderness to Harrison.

Another more civilized outing will take you six miles southeast of Harrison on Highway 65 to the pioneer museum and heritage center located three miles east of Valley Springs. Open daily 9:00 to 5:00 from April 1 to November 30, the museum features a collection honoring the pioneers of the Ozarks. A small fee is charged.

Returning to Highway 65, drive ten miles farther south to explore Hurricane River Cave. Take a guided tour of less than an hour to see the beautiful crystal formations, the rushing underground river, and the many artifacts from centuries ago. Visit the souvenir shop before leaving for St. Joe, ten miles further south.

The primary reason for a stop at St. Joe is a lunch of another delicious Ozark sandwich made from hickory smoked ham, bacon, or summer sausage. Plan an order for a ham to be shipped home or pick up an order blank for later use.

You may retrace your route back to Harrison from St. Joe with enough time to enjoy the beautiful scenery. Or you may wish to explore still farther the backwoods of these beautiful Ozarks. Feel safe to travel one of the unpaved roads of the area.

You might try Highway 235, which leads off Highway 65 approximately 8 miles north of St. Joe. Taking you east towards Yellville, Highway 235 meets Highway 125, which will then lead you northward, back to busy civilization at its junction with Highway 62 between Yellville and Harrison.

To go in the other direction, take Highway 123, which cuts through the Ozark National Forest fifteen miles north of St. Joe. Nine miles southwest on 123 will lead you to the tiny town of Hasty before you cross the waters of the magnificent Buffalo again. About two miles farther south is the junction with Highway 74, which will take you ten miles west to Jasper, where you join Highway 7 for the twenty mile return trip into Harrison. Remember, these roads and backwoods sections are not for the armchair traveler. If you wish to see the Ozarks in their rugged natural state, however, these side trips will delight you.

Take your fishing and boating gear along when you tour the area north of Harrison. Travel along scenic Highway 7 for a fun-filled exploration. A twenty-five mile scenic drive will lead you to the Lead Hill-Diamond City area on the south shores of beautiful Bull Shoals Lake. Noted for its lunker bass fishing, this area also offers white bass, crappie, walleye, bluegill, and the delicious channel cat. Stripers are to be found at weights up to thirty pounds. Lantern fishing at night is very popular. Jump fishing for white bass is good in summer and late fall.

All equipment and guide service is available here in this uncrowded section of the lake, so that you can enjoy all the other water sports also, such as boating, skiing, and swimming. Beyond Diamond City are campgrounds with picnic facilities for your enjoyment as you view the beautiful expanse of blue green waters lapping at this tiny peninsula.

To return to Harrison, take Highway 14 west from Lead Hill. Eight miles of travel will lead you to Highway 281 south, which winds like a corkscrew ten miles to its junction with Highway 7, which will carry you the ten remaining miles to Harrison.

Leaving the Harrison area, travel five miles on Highway 65 north to Bear Creek Springs area. Here you may visit the Bear Creek Springs Trout Farm where you will be treated to a guided tour, showing the growth of the fish from fingerlings to those large enough to be released into the clear waters of Ozark rivers and streams.

From this point, you may continue on Highway 62 to the west and visit the Eureka Springs area. Or turn to the north on Highway 65 leading into the Table Rock Lake area. Either trip will be a fascinating adventure.

TOUR 11

Greers Ferry Area

If you long for the sounds of crickets, frogs, and whippoorwills, then the area around Greers Ferry Lake and Dam is the ideal spot for you. Greers Ferry Lake is stocked full of bass, catfish, crappie, white bass, bream, striped bass, walleye, and chain pickerel. The exotic rainbow trout is found in the lake near the dam and in Little Red River below the dam.

Scuba divers and skin divers find the clear, deep waters ideal. Swimming beaches abound and are well protected from the high speed ski boats and the pleasure craft which crisscross the magnificent waters. This is an extremely popular vacation area of the Ozark Mountains, but with most of the 300-mile shoreline undeveloped, there is still ample space for you to stretch out, relax, and listen to the sounds of nature.

Fees are charged for the campgrounds during the peak season. All offer restrooms, firewood, fireplaces, picnic areas, and water. If you prefer, there are many fine resorts, lodges, motels, hotels, and housekeeping units in the area. Some furnish all water sport needs. Bring your own boat or rent all necessary equipment at any of the commercial marinas on the lake.

As you approach this fascinating area of the Ozarks, be sure to look for the huge round rocks lining the roadways. These are peculiar to this area and were formed from molten lava expelled into the air by volcanic action. The lava then landed in the cold waters, thus forming a perfectly round hollow ball. You should be able to find a small stone to take home as a souvenir.

Greers Ferry Lake can be reached via Arkansas Highways 16, 25, 5, 92, 110, 107, or 225. It is midway between U.S. Highways 65 on the west and 167 on the east. Regardless of your approach, the area will offer golf, tennis, hiking, horseback riding, and all possible water sports.

Sport fishing is in season all year long. In spring, you will find the spawning runs of white bass and walleye. Then the crappie move into the brush tops. An old-fashioned cane pole is ideal for the bream beds you will find in the shallows. Late spring offers you black bass eager for your surface baits. Try your luck at night fishing for the crappie, white bass, or trout in the hot summertime. Fall and winter will bring you easy completion of the limits.

Fish the cold waters of the Little Red below the dam where the rainbow bites on corn, cheese, salmon eggs, worms, or marshmallows. During low water, fly fishing brings your limit of five-pounders and up.

Greers Ferry Lake is divided into two equally beautiful bodies of water. The Narrows is the strip of water connecting the upper and lower sections of the lake. You can find fine fishing and excellent accommodations here.

The small towns of Higden and Greers Ferry are situated on either side of The Narrows and you can spend many enjoyable hours visiting the antique and craft shops in both villages.

Explore a native deer farm. Then take an excursion tour to Sugar Loaf Mountain, which is located in the middle of the upper portion of the lake. Plan to hike up the nature trail for the spectacular view from the mountain top, have a picnic on the island, but most of all, relax and enjoy your visit to this unhurried, unspoiled portion of the Ozarks.

Explore the surrounding area to the north and west of Greers Ferry Lake by traveling Highway 16 past Edgemont to its junction with Highway 330. Turn south on 330 leading into one of the largest recreation-retirement communities in the Ozarks. Every possible accommodation is offered, including the marvelous view of Sugar Loaf Mountain jutting out of the crystal blue waters. The unusual Williams Rock formations are also worth a stop.

Be sure to take a pleasure boat ride on the lake to see the beautiful shoreline. The huge rocks piled one on another form gorgeous backdrops for the lapping blue waters. Moor at one of the many public marinas, hike through the beautiful forests, then picnic in one of the many parks. Photographic subjects abound, so bring lots of film.

To continue your explorations of the area, rejoin Highway 16, traveling north to the town of Shirley. Note the caves that dot the mountain sides along the highway. These were once the homes of the Indians of this area. You may find the nearby Indian Rock House a delightful and inexpensive attraction.

Follow Highway 16 ten miles west to the town of Clinton. Turn north here onto U.S. Highway 65, traveling four miles to the Natural Bridge, a sandstone formation used as a bridge during the eighteenth century. Hike the natural trails leading through the beautiful, rugged woodland. See the moonshine still and the magnificent waterfall.

Watch for signs on the highway leading you to the museum that features early American guns, banks, and music boxes. Open 10:00 to 4:00 daily, the museum is very interesting. Admission is charged.

Farther north on Highway 65 is the fun-filled train ride out over Heartsugg Valley. There is also a zoo and a gift shop.

Then turn back south on Highway 65 and continue past Clinton to the small community of Bee Branch. The scenery along the way is spectacular as you ride the ridges around the blue mountains. The checkerboard of golden sage and green rye meadows stretching out below are magnificent. Turn onto Highway 92 east, which will lead you back into The Narrows area of the lake.

Highway 92 north leads to yet another delightful exploration area. Drive a few short miles past the town of Greers Ferry, cutting off onto the winding road leading down into Frontier Canyon. Stop to swap tales with the artist as you view original paintings depicting local scenes of Ozark natives and their mountains.

Rejoin Highway 92, traveling to the town of Drasco deep in the Ozark hills. Turn into Highway 25 South, which will carry you past Tumbling Shoals into the dam area on the lower edge of Greers Ferry Lake. Be sure to stop for a moment at the Kennedy Memorial, placed at the exact site of the speaker's platform, where President John F. Kennedy made the last official dedication of his life.

Take the free tour of the fish hatchery below the dam. You can see the trout as they advance in size from fingerlings to release size. An aquarium displays all the species of fish found in this area.

Continue on Highway 25 into the small town of Heber Springs. This area has great appeal for vacationers because of its proximity to the lake and its abundance of shops. One of the musts on your visit is a long drink from one of the seven mineral springs located in Spring Park on East Main. Take a leisurely stroll around the town to view some of the quaintly designed older homes. But be sure to return to the park on Saturday nights for the free Hootenanny held in the Amphitheatre during the summer months.

For a real treat, try to visit this area in the fall for the Ozark Frontier Trail Festival and Craft Show, which is held each second full weekend in October. During the three-day festival, you will see in operation a horse-drawn sorghum mill, a

Old-fashioned moonshine still

Natural Bridge (Clinton, Arkansas)

grist mill, and a large spinning wheel producing cotton and wool. There are also exhibitions in weaving on an old-fashioned loom, leather tanning, blacksmithing, basketmaking, wood turning and pottery.

Dollmakers use apple heads, corn shucks, and acorns to make their collector's items. Soap making, broom tying, shingle riving, log splitting, quilting, and natural dyeing of materials from walnuts, sumac, and peach leaves are all demonstrated for your interest and entertainment.

Tap your feet to the folk music programs that emphasize the English and Scotch-Irish ancestry of these mountain settlers. Then help judge the pioneer beard and dress contest prior to the big street dance held in downtown Heber Springs. See the parade of cultural floats and the contests for spinning, horseshoe pitching, and muzzle-loaded rifle firing.

These mountains are beautiful anytime of the year, but fall brings out the most glorious colors. Spring shows its wild plum and pink and white wild dogwoods. Winter bares the hills to allow you a peek inside. And summer enfolds the hills and hollers in lush greens, hiding all their secrets. But no matter what time of year you visit, you will want to take some of the spectacularly beautiful drives through this wonderland.

A short two miles east of Heber Springs on Highway 110 is the foot trail up famed Sugar Loaf Mountain. The panoramic view from the top is well worth the hike up the mountain. Another mile east on Highway 110 brings you to the Winkley Swinging Bridge over the Little Red. This is an excellent fishing hole for rainbow trout. Another 7.2 miles from Swinging Bridge, take the second gravel road on your right. Continue east on the gravel road 6.9 miles to Hiram Church. Across the road from the church is a magnificent overlook view of the Tiny Grand Canyon.

To the south of Heber Springs, turn right on the first gravel road past the Southside Baptist Church. Drive approximately one-half mile to view the ninety foot drop of Bridal Veil Falls. The falls are particularly beautiful during the fall and winter months.

For even more sightseeing in this lovely area of the Ozark Mountains, take a longer drive south on Scenic Highway 5 along the ridges to the tiny hamlet of Rosebud. The road jogs here to continue on to El Paso, deep in an Ozark holler. Here you will find buildings over 100 years old, many with ornate designs and old-time wraparound porches. You might wish to see the 114-year-old church located east of the highway. Circle through the town and return to the highway. Beyond El Paso, the ridges drop to foothills and the golden sage grass covers the rolling plains. Turn onto Highway 64 west, passing through several small towns along the way to the community of Conway.

Turn back onto Highway 65 north at the junction in Conway. Two miles north of Conway is Pickles Gap Creek Crafts, where you can see craftsmen at work on hill country crafts and toys including the famous dancing dolls. Be sure to purchase one of their remarkable "Do-Nothings," an Ozark contraption that accomplishes absolutely nothing. The craftsmen offer buckets, churns, and musical instruments, for your browsing enjoyment.

Continue your travels through the hills and hollows of the foothills to the town of Greenbrier. The more adventurous will want to take the unpaved road 285 into the Woolly Hollow State Park which offers swimming, picnics, snack bar, fishing, nature trails, and more beautiful scenery.

If this does not appeal to you, simply turn onto Highway 25 leading to the town of Quitman. Pass Quitman and take Highway 16 west. Travel 4.2 miles to a gravel road. Turn right here and stay on the main gravel road 5.5 miles to Millers Point. Here you will view one of the more magnificent sights of this area, a panoramic view of thirty miles of Greers Ferry Lake.

Eden Isle, a beautiful outjutting resort area, is to the right and Sugar Loaf Mountain to the far left. Return to Highway 25 and enjoy the beautiful drive back into the main lake area.

Index

Akers Ferry, 77
Albert Pike School House, 18
Alco, Arkansas, 104
Alley Spring Park, 76-77
Allison, Arkansas, 99
Altus, Arkansas, 21
Alum Cove, 111
Anderson, Missouri, 45
Appletown, U.S.A. 11-12
Aquarium, 53, 118
Arkansas Gun Club, 84
Arkansas River, 18, 19
Arkansas Traveller Folk Theatre, 88
Artist Point, 17
Ash Flat, 89
Aurora, Missouri, 48
Ava, Missouri, 70

Bagnell Dam, 53, 58
Bartlett, Missouri, 77, 79
Basin Park Hotel, 24
Batesville, Arkansas, 104-105
Battlefields, 9, 12, 13-14, 28, 51, 69
Bear Creek Springs, 113
Beaver Lake, 13, 14, 27
Bella Vista, Arkansas, 16
Bennett Springs State Park, 62
Bentonville, Arkansas, 16
Berryville, Arkansas, 30
Big Flat, Arkansas, 103

Big Piney River, 69
Big Spring Park, 45
Big Springs Park, 78
Big Sugar Creek, 32
Birch Tree, Missouri, 77, 79
Black River, 74
Blanchard Springs, 102
Blanchard Springs Caverns, 99-102
Blue Spring, 27, 74, 90
Bluff Dwellers Cave, 16, 46
Bolivar, Simon, 70
Booger Hollow, Arkansas, 111-112
Boston Mountains, 16
Branson, Missouri, 32-35
Bridal Cave, 56-57
Bridal Veil Falls, 121
Brockwell, Arkansas, 104
Bruno, Arkansas, 95
Buffalo National Recreational Point 93
Buffalo National River, 93, 103, 105, 110
Bull Shoals Caverns, 83
Bull Shoals Lake, 41-42, 80-82, 83, 89, 113
Bull Shoals State Park, 82
Butterfield Stage, 9, 14, 17

Cabool, Missouri, 69
Calico Rock, Arkansas, 104
Camdenton, Missouri, 56, 57, 60

Cane Hill, Arkansas, 12
Caney Refuge, 90
Canoeing. *See* Floating Trips
Cardareva Cave, 75
Carrie Nation Hatchet Hall, 24
Carroll County Museum, 30
Carthage, Missouri, 49-50; Battle of, 51
Carver, George Washington, 44-45
Cassville, Missouri, 40
Castle, 27
Caves, 16, 17, 30, 31, 34, 39, 40, 45-46, 55, 56-57, 63-66, 68, 75-76, 83, 93, 99-102, 109- 110, 117
Cave Spring, 76
Cherokee Indians, 10, 27
Chesapeake hatchery, 48
Christ of the Ozarks (statue), 30
Christ Only Art Gallery, 30
Church in the Wildwood, 28
Civil War, 9, 10, 12, 13-14, 16, 25, 49, 50, 51, 63, 66, 69, 70, 87
Civil War Cave, 16
Civil War National Cemetery, 70
Clarksville, Arkansas, 21
Clear Creek, 50
Climax Springs, Missouri, 60
Clinton, Arkansas, 117
Cole County, Historical Museum, 60
Confederate Cemetery, 10
Conway, Arkansas, 121
Cosmic Cavern, 31
Cotter, Arkansas, 82, 84
Crafts, 10, 12, 14-16, 17-18, 25, 33, 34-35, 39, 41, 42, 45, 53, 55, 81, 88, 91, 97-98, 99, 109-110, 121
Crescent Hotel, 22, 31
Crooked Creek, 80, 91
Crystal Cave, 68
Crystal Caverns, 40
Cuba, Missouri, 66

Cula Vista, Missouri, 39
Current River, 73, 75, 76, 77, 78

Dawt Mill, 90-91
Devil's Den State Park, 17, 21
Devil's Well, 76
Dewey Bald Mountain, 35
Diamond, Missouri, 45
Diamond Cave, 110
Diamond City, Arkansas, 113
Dinosaur Park, 28
Dogpatch, U.S.A., 108-109
Dogpatch Caverns, 109
Drasco, Arkansas, 118
Driftwood, Jimmy, 104
Drury College, 68
Dry Nob Mill, 67

Eagle Rock, 41
Eden Isle, 122
Eldon, Missouri, 55, 58
El Dorado Springs, 50
Eleven Point River, 78
Elkhorn Tavern, 14, 28
Elk River, 46, 48
El Paso, Arkansas, 121
Emerald Grotto, 75
Eminence, Missouri, 73
Eureka Springs, Arkansas, 22-25, 31, 113

Fairs and festivals, 10, 11, 12, 14-16, 21, 30, 31, 34-35, 42, 45, 57, 72, 77, 89-90, 91, 97, 98-99, 103, 104, 105, 107, 118-20
Falling Spring and Mill, 78
Falls Creek, 37
Fantastic Caverns, 68
Fayetteville, Arkansas, 9-10; Battle of, 9
Festivals. *See* Fairs and Festivals
Fifty-Six, 103
Fisher Pond and Mines, 78-79

124

Fisher's Cave, 66
Fishing, 13, 27-28, 36, 37, 40, 41, 46, 49, 50, 55, 57, 58, 67, 69, 70-72, 76, 77, 78, 81-82, 83-84, 86, 87-88, 104, 113, 115, 116
Floating trips, 51, 62, 66, 69, 72, 73, 76, 77, 82, 86, 91, 93, 103, 110
Forsyth, Missouri, 42
Fort Smith, Arkansas, 18
Frontier Canyon, 118
Frontier Trail Festival and Craft Show, 118-20

Gainesville, Missouri, 89-90
Gaither Mountain Park, 111
Gasconade River, 67
Gassville, Arkansas, 84
George Washington Carver National Monument, 44-45
Ghost town, 17, 98, 104
Golf, 16, 55
Grape Festival, 11
Great Passion Play, 30
Greenbrier, Arkansas, 121
Greenfield Museum, 51
Greers Ferry, Arkansas, 116, 118
Greers Ferry Lake and Dam, 115-17, 118, 121-22
Greer Spring and Mill, 78
Guion, Arkansas, 105
Gun Club. *See* Arkansas Gun Club
Gunner pool area, 102-103

"Hanging Judge," 18
Hardy, Arkansas, 88
Harrison, Arkansas, 107, 112, 113
Hasty, Arkansas, 112
Hatchery, 37, 58, 84-86, 87, 113, 118
Headquarters House, 9
Heartsugg Valley, 117
Heber Springs, 118-20
Higden, Arkansas, 116

Hiking, 13, 17, 74, 93, 110-11, 116, 120
Hiram Church, 120
Historical Museum (Eureka Springs, Arkansas), 24
Hodgson Mill, 90
Hog Scald Hollow, 25
Horseshoe Bend, Arkansas, 89
Hunting, 13, 45, 50, 67, 69, 81, 86, 90, 98
Hurricane River Cave, 112

Indian Burial Cave, 60
Indian Rock House, 117
International Air Gun Museum, 13

Jacks Fork River, 73, 75
Jacobs Cave, 55
James, Jesse, 63, 66
Jasper, Arkansas, 110, 112
Jasper County Courthouse, 49
Jefferson City, Missouri, 60
Johnson's Shut Ins State Park, 74
Jolly Mill, 49
Joplin, Missouri, 44

Kaiser Tower, 58
Kennedy Memorial, 118
Kimberling City, Missouri, 40
Kings River, 30

LaJolla Park, 66
Lake Fort Smith, 18
Lake Leatherwood, 27
Lake Norfork, 80, 86-87, 91
Lake of the Ozarks, 52-56, 58
Lake of the Ozarks State Park, 57-58
Lake Shepherd Springs, 18
Lake Taneycomo, 37, 42-43
Lakeview, Missouri, 81-82
Lamar, Missouri, 50
Lanagan, Missouri, 45
Laurie, Missouri, 56

Lead Hill, Arkansas, 113
Lebanon, Missouri, 62
Leslie, Arkansas, 103-104
Lesterville, Missouri, 74
Licking, Missouri, 66
Lincoln, Arkansas, 11
Little Red River, 103, 116, 120
Logan Creek Mine, 74
Lone Pine, Arkansas, 103
Lost Valley State Park, 110-11

Majorville, Missouri, 60
Mammoth Spring State Park, 87-88
Mansfield, Missouri, 69
Many Islands Camp Grounds, 88
Mark Twain National Forest, 40, 42, 78, 90
Marshall, Arkansas, 103, 105
Marvel Cave, 34
Mason-Dixon Line, 46-48
Matney Campground, 82-83
Melbourne, Arkansas, 104, 105
Meramac Caverns, 63
Meramac State Park, 63
Midway, Arkansas, 81
Millers Point, 121
Mills, 12, 37, 49, 66, 67, 69, 76, 78, 90-91, 102, 105, 118-20
Mining, 44, 74, 78
Missouri Aquarium, 53
Missouri State Highway Patrol Museum, 60
Monett, Missouri, 48
Montauk State Park, 75
Morgan County Museum, 55
Morning Star, Arkansas, 103
Mountain Grove, 69
Mountain Home, Arkansas, 80-81, 83, 84, 86
Mountain View, Arkansas, 77, 96-99
Mountain Village, 1890, 83
Mt. Olive, 104

Mount Shira Cave, 46
Mt. Vernon, Missouri, 48
Museums, 10-11, 12, 13, 16, 17, 18, 24, 25-27, 30, 35, 37, 44, 45, 49, 50, 51, 55, 60, 66, 89, 105, 107, 112, 117
Music, 12, 24, 25-27, 34, 35, 48, 69, 75, 84, 87, 98, 104, 107, 118

Narrows, 66, 116, 118
Nation, Carrie, 24
National Festival of Craftsmen, 34-35
National Register of Historic Places, 10, 22, 31
Neosho, Missouri, 45
Nevada, Missouri, 50
New Orleans Hotel, 31
Niangua River, 57, 62, 70
Nixa, Missouri, 69
Noel, Missouri, 16, 46
Norfork, Arkansas, 84
Norfork Dam, 84-86
Norfork River, 84
North Fork River, 86

Old Spanish Cave, 39
Old Spring Mill, 105
Onondaga Cave, 63
Onyx Cave, 30
Osage Beach, 56, 57
Osage Fork River, 67
Osage Indians, 58
Osage River, 58
Ozarks Arts and Crafts Fair, 14-16
Ozark Folk Center, 96-99
Ozark Folk Festival, 31, 96, 97
Ozark Frontier Trail, 49, 75, 81, 87, 89
Ozark National Forest, 11, 18, 19, 21, 73-74, 99-103, 104, 111, 112

Ozark National Scenic Riverways, 73
Ozarks Caverns, 58
Ozark Wonder Cave, 46
Oxley, Arkansas, 104

Paradise Hill, Arkansas, 109-10
Parker, Judge Isaac C., 18
Passion Play, 30
Pea Ridge National Military Park, 13-14, 28
Peel, 83-84
Penrod Museum, 81
Pickles Gap Creek, 121
Pierce City, Missouri, 48-49
Pike, Albert, 18
Pilot Point, 87
Pineville, Missouri, 46
Piney River, 66, 67, 69
Pomme de Terre River, 58, 70, 72
Pomme de Terre State Park, 72
Ponca, Arkansas, 110
Powder Mill Ferry, 73-74
Prairie Grove Battlefield Park, 12
Prairie Grove Clothesline Fair, 12
Prairie Hollow Cave, 58
Pulltite Spring, 76

Quitman, Arkansas, 121

Rainbow Springs Trout Farm, 91
Ralph, Arkansas, 91
Reeds Spring Junction, 39
Reiff House, 10
Ridge House, 10
Ritchey Mill, 49
Roaring River State Park, 28, 40-41
Rockaway Beach, Missouri, 42
Rockbridge Mill, 90
Rock Collecting, 81, 83, 84, 115-16
Rocky Falls, 77
Rogers, Arkansas, 9, 13

Rolla, Missouri, 66
Rosalie, 24
Rosebud, Arkansas, 121
Roubidoux Spring and Creek, 67
Round Spring Caverns, 75
Round Spring Park, 75
Rush, Arkansas, 93

St. Elizabeth's Catholic Church, 22
St. Joe, Arkansas, 112
St. Mary's Mountain, 19
Salem, Arkansas, 87, 89
Saunders Memorial Museum, 30
Schaberg, Arkansas, 17
School of the Ozarks, 37
Scuba Diving, 36, 41, 82, 86, 115
SEFOR Nuclear Experiment Station, 17
Seven Springs, 76
Shannondale, Missouri, 76
Shawnee Cave, 93
Shepherd of the Hills, The (Wright), 35-36
Shepherd of the Hills Farm, 36-37
Shiloh Museum, 10
Shirley, Arkansas, 117
Shoal Creek, 49, 51
Shore Lake, 19
Siloam Springs, Arkansas, 11
Silver Dollar City, 32-35
Sinks, The, 75-76
Snowball, Arkansas, 105
Southwest City, Missouri, 46
Springdale, Arkansas, 9, 12, 14, 16
Springfield, Missouri, 67, 68-69
Spring River, 48, 49-50, 87-88
Starks Cave, 55
Starr, Belle, 18, 49
Steelville, Missouri, 66
Stockton, Missouri, 72
Stockton Lake, 50, 70
Stockton State Park, 70
Stover, Missouri, 58

Strawberry Festival, 103
Sugar Loaf Mountain, 116, 120, 122
Sunk Lands, The, 77
Sylamore, Arkansas, 99, 105

Table Rock Lake, 28, 36, 37, 40, 41, 114
Talimena Skyline Drive, 17
Talking Rocks Cavern, 39
Three Brothers, Missouri, 89
Timbo, Arkansas, 104
Tiny Grand Canyon, 120
Tontitown, Arkansas, 11
Topaz Mill, 69
Top O' The Ozarks Tower, 83
"Trail of Tears," 27
Tri-State Mineral Museum, 44
Truitt's Cave, 45-46
Truman, Harry S., 50
Turkey Trot, 91
Twin Creeks, Arkansas, 104
Two Rivers Ferry, 75

Underground Railroad, 63
U. S. Weather Radar Station, 48
University of Arkansas, 10

Valley Springs, Arkansas, 112
Van Buren, Arkansas, 18
Van Buren, Missouri, 78
Versailles, Missouri, 55, 58

War Eagle Mills Farm, 14
Welch Spring, 76
White River, 28, 82-83, 84, 104
White River Museum, 43
White River Water Carnival, 105
Wilder, Laura Ingalls, 69
Wilderness Road, 39
Wilson's Creek National Battlefield, 69
Winkley Swinging Bridge, 120
Winona, Missouri, 77, 78
Withrow Springs State Park, 25
Witts Spring, Arkansas, 105
Wolf House, 84
Woolly Hollow State Park, 121
Wright, Harold Bell, 35, 36, 49

Yancy Mills, 66
Yellville, Arkansas, 83, 91, 112

Zanoni Mill, 90